D0793852

Voyages to Hawaii before 1860

LIBRARY

APR 1 5 1975

UNIVERSITY OF HAWAII

Voyages to Hawaii before 1860

A Record, Based on Historical Narratives in the Libraries of the Hawaiian Mission Children's Society and The Hawaiian Historical Society, Extended to March 1860

Bernice Judd

enlarged and edited by Helen Yonge Lind

THE UNIVERSITY PRESS OF HAWAII

for

HAWAIIAN MISSION CHILDREN'S SOCIETY

Honolulu

LIBRARY

APR 1 5 1975

UNIVERSITY OF THE PACIFIC

294150

This edition is a revision of that originally published in 1929 by the Hawaiian Mission Children's Society.

Copyright © 1974 by The University Press of Hawaii

All rights reserved

Library of Congress Catalog Card Number 74–78864

ISBN 0–8248–0329–9

Manufactured in the United States of America

IN MEMORY OF BERNICE JUDD

The earlier edition of this book, published in 1929, was written by Bernice Judd. She kept two interleaved copies in which she noted further entries during her thirty-three years' work in the Hawaiian Mission Children's Society library. Her work there was described in a resolution adopted by the Society soon after her death on March 12, 1971:

> Curious Cousins, would-be historians, ambitious thesis-writers, famous novelists, and distinguished scholars—all of them she guided with a sure hand, a gracious manner, and a contagious enthusiasm. Always meticulous and thorough, always committed to historical truth, she won the confidence of the skeptical, unsnarled tangles for the confused, and spiced the day's work with her incomparable sense of humor.

With gratitude and affection, the Hawaiian Mission Children's Society dedicates this edition to Bernice Judd.

CONTENTS

The Hawaiian Mission Children's Society received several contributions in Bernice Judd's memory, and decided that a new edition would be the fitting memorial because it would not merely commemorate Bernice Judd, but would perpetuate her work for future generations of historians and other scholars. Her friends contributed further to help defray the costs of publication.

This edition is primarily an enlargement rather than a revised version of Miss Judd's original book. Her work was so meticulous that despite discoveries of other researchers during the intervening forty-five years, very few changes in factual information were necessary. Some attempt was made to simplify the punctuation, and the bibliographic descriptions have been revamped to modern standards. Otherwise Miss Judd's text is for the most part intact and all new entries were composed in somewhat the same style and character as the original compilation.

In her Preface, Miss Judd explained that her study was limited to the material in the library of the Hawaiian Mission Children's Society. Information gathered from all qualifying publications acquired by the Society after 1929 has been added. In addition a number of volumes from the library of The Hawaiian Historical Society were researched. Since 1950, the collections of these two societies have been housed and used together as "The Mission-Historical Library."

All entries in the Bibliography (Section 3) in the first edition were arranged alphabetically by author, then numbered consecutively. This arrangement has been retained. All added entries have been placed in their proper sequence and given the number of the preceding entry followed by a letter, such as 19a, 84b, and so forth.

The most conspicuous change is a three-month extension of the original closing date, which was January 1, 1860. This was done to include views of life in Hawaii through the eyes of Asians, members of the first Japanese embassy to the United States, which visited Honolulu in March of 1860.

HELEN YONGE LIND

Advisory Committee
Clare G. Murdoch, *chairman*
Janet E. Bell
Agnes C. Conrad
Elizabeth A. Larsen

No list of voyages to Hawaii has appeared in book form since the interesting group of Hawaiian bibliography was published in the 1860s. First came W. Harper Pease's *Catalogue of Works Relating to the Hawaiian or Sandwich Islands*. As a pamphlet of twenty-four pages, it was published in Honolulu in 1862. It may be found also in *The Friend* for May and June 1862. Then followed William Martin's *Catalogue d'Ouvrages Relatif aux Iles Hawaii* . . . , published in Paris in 1867. It is a bibliography arranged by subject with a large section devoted to voyages. The Hawaiian Club founded in Boston by a few men interested in these islands published among its papers in 1868 a bibliography of the Hawaiiana then known to its members. A short list of voyages is given, arranged chronologically with the author and year of visit only. The following year, 1869, James Hunnewell had this bibliography of the Club privately printed.

It has seemed worthwhile to reexamine this subject of voyages to Hawaii, although a complete enumeration of the vessels has not been attempted in the present publication. While a complete list is desirable, to accomplish such a study, it would be necessary to examine carefully all the known ships' logs, private journals, newspapers, and other old documents.

Arbitrary lines had to be drawn. It was decided to limit the study to the material in the library of the Hawaiian Mission Children's Society. This view is a broad one, for the library is one of the largest of Hawaiiana in existence. After collecting for over a decade, Mr. George R. Carter in 1920 gave the library, together with an endowment, to the Society.

Certain volumes known to be in other libraries in Honolulu have not been included, without materially impairing, it is believed, the value of this study. For instance, while the official edition of Freycinet's expedition is owned by The Hawaiian Historical Society, that voyage is recorded in the library of the Hawaiian Mission Children's Society by the account written by Jacques Arago, the draftsman. Similarly, there have been used only those diaries kept by the American missionaries in their perilous journeys around the Horn which happen to be in this library, although there are many such journals of these and other voyages present in Honolulu outside of libraries and not yet readily accessible.

Another arbitrary decision was made to limit the study to source material. Therefore, many books in the library have not been used. There have been omitted such secondary accounts as *An Historical Account of the Circumnavigation of the Globe . . . from the Voyage of Magellan to the Death of Cook* (Second edition. Edinburgh, 1837). Only those editions of a book have been named which were consulted for information. For instance, although the library possesses five editions of Archibald Campbell's *Voyages*, only one, the earliest, has been cited, for that one reports fully the facts of Campbell's arrival and departure. On the other hand, two editions of Ellis' *Polynesian Researches* have been noted because each has details not found in the other. Autobiographies have been included as source material; but biographies in general have been omitted unless in them has been found information not available elsewhere. *The Lives of Penrose and Trevenen,* a biography written by John Penrose, their nephew, is a case in point. Although Trevenen was with Captain Cook on his third voyage, the portion of this book which deals with Hawaii adds nothing of value to this study.

"Voyage" is defined as "a journey by water, especially by sea." It may be used to mean either one or both of the outward and homeward passages of a vessel. This is not always the case, however. A person may arrive on one boat and leave on another.

The year 1860 was chosen as a natural boundary or limit. By that year the government was on a firm basis; the independence of the Hawaiian monarchy had been recognized fully by the foreign powers. The whaling industry had begun to decline. The American Board of Commissioners for Foreign Missions was retiring from its direct control over its mission in these islands.

The limit set by the year 1860 caused certain books to be omitted. Among these are *Japan, the Amoor and the Pacific* by Tilley (London, 1861) and *The Cruise of the Cachelot* by Bullen (New York, 1899). Tilley, on his way to Japan on board the Russian corvette *Rynda,* reached Honolulu on January 16, 1860. This date of arrival makes his visit just too late to be placed on this list. Bullen gives no dates in his book, but as the Library of Congress card states 1857 as the date of his birth, and as he says he was eighteen at the beginning of the cruise, his visit to Hawaii must have been about 1875.

A "historical narrative" is used here to mean any book which gives an orderly continuous account of the successive particulars of an event or a series of events which actually happened. Nevertheless, when there has been doubt about a book's coming in this classification, it has been included; as for instance, *Journal of a Tour on the North West Coast of America in 1829* by J. S. Green. For the purpose of this study, official government reports and documents were not considered "historical narratives." This explains the omission of such publications as the de Tromelin Treaty of 1840 and the records of the litigation over the *William Little*. A few books are clearly not "historical narratives" of Hawaii. *Aleck: the Last of the Mutineers* (Boston, 1848) is an example. Aleck was one of the mutineers of the *Bounty*. The account barely mentions that he visited the Hawaiian Islands, but the vessels and dates are not given. Hall, in his book, *Arctic Rovings* (Boston, 1861), tells merely of the comings and goings of a whaling voyage, incidentally inventing the phenomenon of a volcanic eruption at Honolulu in 1858! No item has been placed in the bibliography unless it possesses something of interest about a period of Hawaiian history. Every book contains something more than the bare fact that a boat came here and departed. It must have some comment on the life and customs in these islands or mention of an event which colored the history of Hawaii. No effort has been made to exclude opinions which are prejudiced and consequently do not give a true account; for it has been recognized that they are of interest to the student who is attempting to gain an insight into the spirit of a period.

The voyages are shown in a chronological list of vessels. Such information about each vessel or voyage as was judged pertinent has been noted. In many cases it has been difficult to obtain exact dates. Sometimes an author states merely the year and that he "stayed three months." Again, no year is given but a careful reading of the text reveals the period in which the visit must have been made. Rev. Henry Cheever in his book, *The Island World of the Pacific*, neglects to mention any dates, but his arrival at these islands must have been after August 1849,[*] for he describes "the fort, which the French, under Admiral Tromelin, have recently dismantled." Sometimes there has been more than one date from which to choose the precise day that a boat reached Hawaii, because, after sighting land, sailing vessels often took several days to reach a harbor in which they might anchor. Whenever there has been a possible choice, the date of anchorage has been selected. For example, April 4, 1820 has been given for the arrival of the brig *Thaddeus*, the day the vessel anchored in Kailua Bay, although she had sighted Mauna Kea on March 30.

It is known that certain vessels and persons have made visits of which no "historical narratives" are in this library. A few of these have been included because of their historical importance, it being obvious that the omission of such visits as Paulet's in 1843 and de Tromelin's in 1849 would impair the usefulness of this publication to those who may turn to it for information. The historical significance of voyages thus incorporated has been based largely on the authority of *A Brief History of the Hawaiian People* by W. D. Alexander. Each item added in this way has been marked with an asterisk (*).

An alphabetical list has been prepared of all the names of individuals and vessels appearing in the chronological list. When known, the status and nationality of each person have been given; likewise, the vessels on which they traveled, but with only the year of their arrival. Similarly, the registry and type of vessel have

---

* Cheever arrived in 1843 but did not publish his book until 1851. H.Y.L.

been given with its master or commander and the year of its visit. These details are sufficient for easy reference to the chronological list where additional information of the visit may be found.

The bibliography is numbered and arranged alphabetically by authors. For the most part, it consists of "historical narratives." However, certain books have been included which were used to supply the omissions in the "historical narratives" of dates and other desired information. These books are *The Friend, The Missionary Herald, Sandwich Island Gazette, The Polynesian,* Bingham's *Residence of Twenty-One Years,* certain volumes of Bancroft's *History, Minutes of the General Meetings,* Kuykendall's and Gregory's *History of Hawaii,* Alexander's *Brief History,* and Judge F. W. Howay's *Address* delivered during the Cook Sesquicentennial Celebration. The last item has been included because it describes many of the vessels which came to Hawaii before 1800 and concerning which little has been known. It is understood that this paper will be published in the near future, together with the other addresses of the Sesquicentennial held in Hawaii in August 1928 under the auspices of the Territory.[*]

Neither the time nor the material at hand has made it possible in every instance to achieve completeness. Spaces have been left so that the users of this pamphlet may add details. In the cases of two or more vessels with the same name visiting Hawaii at different periods, no special effort has been made to determine if such boats are identical. Therefore, questions arise for others to answer. For instance, was the *Vincennes,* Captain Finch, which came here in 1829, the same *Vincennes* which was Commodore Wilkes' flag ship in 1840? Again, were the three *Columbias* which apparently belonged to the Hudson Bay Company three different ships? It is entirely possible that the company used that name for more than one boat, though it does not seem probable. The United States frigate *Columbia* and the other *Columbias* of earlier date are not likely to be confused. Similarly, it has not been possible to check the identity of men of the same name arriving in different years. These names have been recorded as they appear. However, in those few cases where the evidence

---

* Published in 1930. See Section III, Bibliography, number 84. H.Y.L.

seemed convincing, the men have been treated as identical and a note made to that effect in the alphabetical list.

In an attempt to assist those who are interested in illustrations of early Hawaii, the number of engravings, woodcuts, and lithographs pertaining to these islands has been added after each item in the bibliography. In those instances where the engravings in one edition are unlike those in another, both editions have been listed. For example, the four items by Jacques Arago have been cited because the engravings in each appear to have been printed from different plates. In this effort there have been omitted those books which, although they have engravings, are not "historical narratives of voyages to Hawaii," as Dibble's *History* and Jarves' *History*. Although William Ellis' *Journal of a Tour* has several engravings from sketches by the author, it has not been noted because it is an account of a journey within these islands.

It is hoped that this book will be of service not only to those who are interested in voyages to Hawaii in particular, but also to those who may wish to know more about the fascinating early days of Hawaiian history.

To those who have assisted with their time and information in the preparation of this study, grateful appreciation is made.

BERNICE JUDD.

Chronological List of Vessels

All numbers enclosed in brackets
([ ]) refer to items in the bibliography.
An asterisk (*) signifies there is no
"historical narrative" in the
library. See pages xv–xvi.

1778, 1779

Resolution—H.B.M. sloop, 452 tons, Capt. James Cook in command; arrived January 18, 1778, departed February 2, 1778.
Discovery, Clerke, was in company. Cook discovered the
Hawaiian Islands on this, his third voyage of discovery, and
named them the Sandwich Islands in honor of his patron,
the Earl of Sandwich.

Second visit—Arrived November 26, 1778, departed February 4, 1779; but a broken mast on the *Resolution* forced
both vessels to return February 11, 1779. Capt. Cook was
killed on February 14. Both vessels finally left islands March
13, 1779, Capt. Clerke in command of *Resolution* and Capt.
Gore of *Discovery*. Capt. Clerke died of consumption soon
afterwards. Then Capt. Gore commanded *Resolution* and
Capt. King the *Discovery*. [44, 44a, 59, 64a, 74, 108, 150,
157, 193, 193a]

Discovery—H.B.M. sloop, 300 tons, Capt. Charles Clerke, accompanied *Resolution*, Capt. James Cook.

1786

King George—British registry, 320 tons, Capt. Nathaniel Portlock;
arrived May 24, 1786, departed June 13, 1786; accompanied
by *Queen Charlotte*, Dixon; trading voyage between west
coast of America and China. [136, 147]

King George came a second time in November 1786 and a third time in September 1787.

Queen Charlotte—British registry, 200 tons, Capt. George Dixon, with Portlock's expedition; arrived May 26, 1786, departed June 13, 1786; accompanied *King George;* trading voyage between west coast of America and China. [53]

Queen Charlotte came a second time in November 1786 and a third time in September 1787.

Boussole—French naval frigate, La Pérouse in command; arrived May 29, 1786, departed May 30, 1786. *Astrolabe* was in company. La Pérouse landed at Maui only. [102, 103, 104]

Astrolabe—French naval frigate, de Langle in command, with La Pérouse's expedition; arrived May 29, 1786, departed May 30, 1786; accompanied *Boussole*. [102, 103, 104]

King George—British registry, 320 tons, Capt. Nathaniel Portlock; arrived November 16, 1786, departed March 3, 1787; accompanied by *Queen Charlotte*, Dixon; trading voyage between west coast of America and China. [136, 147]

King George came first in May 1786 and a third time in September 1787.

Queen Charlotte—British registry, 200 tons, Capt. George Dixon; with Portlock's expedition; arrived November 16, 1786, departed March 15, 1787; accompanied *King George;* trading voyage between west coast of America and China. [53]

Queen Charlotte came first in May 1786 and a third time in September 1787.

1787

Nootka—British registry, 200 tons, John Meares, master; arrived August 2, 1787, departed September 2, 1787; Meares' first visit; Kaiana (Tianna) a passenger for China. [121, 122, 123]

Queen Charlotte—British registry, 200 tons, Capt. George Dixon; with Portlock's expedition; arrived September 5, 1787, departed September 18, 1787; trading voyage between west coast of America and China. [53]

Queen Charlotte made two earlier visits to Hawaii, arriving in May and September 1786.

King George—British registry, 320 tons, Capt. Nathaniel Portlock;

arrived September 27, 1787, departed October 8, 1787; trading voyage between west coast of America and China. [136, 147]

King George made two earlier visits to Hawaii, arriving in May and September 1786.

* *Imperial Eagle* or *Loudoun*—"British ship flying Austrian colors," 400 tons, in fur trade; Charles William Barkley, master; arrived May 20, 1787, departed May 25, 1787. [84]

1788

Prince of Wales—British registry, ship, 171 tons, trader, Capt. James Colnett, master; arrived January 2, 1788, departed March 18, 1788. [40a, 84a]

Princess Royal—British registry, sloop, 65 tons, trader, Capt. Charles Duncan, master; companion vessel to the *Prince of Wales;* arrived January 2, 1788, departed March 18, 1788. [40a, 84a]

Felice—British registry, 230 tons, John Meares, master; arrived October 18, 1788, departed October 26, 1788; Meares' second visit. [121, 122, 123]

Iphigenia—British registry, ship, 200 tons, William Douglas, master; arrived December 6, 1788, Kaiana (Tianna) a passenger; departed March 15, 1789; accompanied by *North West America*. [121, 122, 123]

Iphigenia returned later in 1789.

North West America—British registry, schooner, 40 tons, Robert Funter, master; arrived December 6, 1788, departed March 15, 1789; accompanied *Iphigenia*. [121, 122, 123]

1789

Iphigenia—British registry, 200 tons, William Douglas, master; arrived July 20, 1789, departed August 20, 1789. [121, 122, 123]

Iphigenia visited Hawaii in 1788–1789 also.

* *Columbia*—Boston registry, ship, 250 tons, Robert Gray, master; arrived in August of 1789, departed _____; trader, first American vessel to circumnavigate the globe. [98]

Mercury—British registry, brig, 152 tons, Capt. John Henry Cox, master; arrived September 23, 1789, departed September 25, 1789; George Mortimer on board. [131]

1790

* *Eleanora*—American registry, brig, Simon Metcalf, master; 1790. By ordering the Olowalu Massacre, Simon Metcalf provoked the natives to retaliation. This the Hawaiians accomplished by capturing the *Fair American* and killing all the crew except Isaac Davis. When John Young, the boatswain, was sent ashore from the *Eleanora* a few days later, he was held by the natives for fear he would tell Metcalf of the fate of the crew of the *Fair American*. Young and Davis became two of Kamehameha I's chief advisors. [1, 98a]
* *Fair American*—American registry, Thomas Metcalf, master; 1790; tender of *Eleanora*. [2, 98a]
Grace—American schooner, 85 tons, William Douglas, owner and master; arrived and departed about September 1790. [84a, 87]

1791

Princess Royal—formerly British registry, sloop, 65 tons, captured by the Spaniards in 1789 and now under Spanish colors, Manuel Quimper, master. Sighted Hawaii March 20 and anchored March 23, 1791, sailed for Manila April 18, 1791. [148a]
* *Argonaut*—British registry, merchant vessel, James Colnett, master; arrived April 1791, departed ———; credited with bringing first sheep to Kauai. *See* Colnett, James.
Hope—American registry, brigantine, trader, Joseph Ingraham, master; arrived May 20, 1791, departed May 29, 1791. [87] *Hope* returned in October of 1791.
Gustavus III—formerly the British snow *Mercury* but "flying Swedish colors," 152 tons, Capt. Thomas Barnett, master; John Bartlett, seaman, aboard; arrived August 22, 1791, departed September 1, 1791. [13a]
Solide—French registry, 300 tons, Étienne Marchand in command;

made Hawaii October 4, 1791; passed Kauai October 10, 1791; did not anchor. [68]

Hope—American registry, brigantine, trader, Joseph Ingraham, master; arrived October 6, 1791, departed October 12, 1791. [87]

> *Hope* visited Hawaii first in May of 1791.

* *Lady Washington*—American registry, brigantine (formerly a sloop), 90 tons, Capt. John Kendrick, master; arrived and departed October–November 1791. [1, 84, 84a, 98, 98a]

> *Lady Washington* was here again in 1793 and 1794.

* *Hancock*—American registry, brig, Capt. Samuel Crowell, master; arrived _____ 1791, departed _____. [84, 84a]

1792

Discovery—H.B.M. sloop, 350 tons, Capt. George Vancouver, on a voyage of discovery; accompanied by *Chatham;* arrived March 2, 1792, departed March 16, 1792. Archibald Menzies, naturalist and surgeon, Thomas Manby, master's mate, aboard. [116a, 125, 178, 179]

> *Discovery* came again in 1793 and 1794.

Chatham—H.B.M. armed tender, 135 tons, Lieut. William Robert Broughton; accompanied *Discovery*, Vancouver; arrived March 2, 1792, departed March 16, 1792. Edward Bell, clerk, aboard. [18a, 178, 179]

> *Chatham* came again in 1793 and 1794.

Daedalus—British naval store ship, Lieut. Hergest, brought supplies for Vancouver; arrived May 7, 1792, departed May 12, 1792. On May 11, Lieut. Hergest and two others were killed by the natives at Waimea, Oahu. [179]

Columbia—Boston registry, ship, 250 tons, Robert Gray, master; arrived October 29, 1792, departed November 3, 1792; John Boit, Jr., fifth mate. [24]

> *Columbia* touched at Hawaii in 1789.

* *Halcyon*—_____ registry, Charles William Barkley, master; arrived November 8, 1792, departed November 15, 1792. [84, 84a]

* *Margaret*—American registry, ship, Capt. Magee, master; arrived _____ 1792, departed _____. [84, 84a]

* *Jenny*—"of Bristol, England," three-masted schooner, Capt. Baker, master; arrived _____ 1792, departed _____; captured two natives who were returned by Vancouver the next year. [84, 84a]

1793

* *Jackal*—British registry, schooner or cutter, Alexander Stewart, master; arrived February 1793, departed _____ 1793. [2, 98a]
  Jackal returned later in the year.
Discovery—H.B.M. sloop, 350 tons, Capt. George Vancouver, on a voyage of exploration, accompanied by *Chatham*, Puget; arrived February 12, 1793, departed March 30, 1793; Archibald Menzies, surgeon and naturalist. [125, 178, 179]
  Discovery had come in 1792 and came again in 1794.
Chatham—H.B.M. armed tender, 135 tons, Lieut. Peter Puget; accompanied *Discovery*, Vancouver; arrived February 12, 1793, departed March 16, 1793. Edward Bell, clerk, and Thomas Manby, master's mate, aboard. [18a, 116a, 178, 179]
  Chatham had come in 1792 and came again in 1794.
* *Butterworth*—English registry, trader, William Brown, master; arrived February 1793, departed _____ 1793. *Butterworth* returned later in the year about November, and was sent back to England. Capt. William Brown transferred to the *Jackal*. [2, 98a] For a discussion of Capt. Brown, *see* "A Northwest Trader at the Hawaiian Islands" by Ralph S. Kuykendall, in *Quarterly of the Oregon Historical Society*, vol. 24, pp. 111–131.
* *Jefferson*—American registry, ship, Capt. Josiah Roberts, master; arrived March 1793, departed _____. [84, 84a]
  Jefferson came again in 1794.
* *Lady Washington*—American registry, brigantine (formerly a sloop), 90 tons, Capt. John Kendrick, master; arrived October–November, 1793, departed Spring 1794. [2, 84, 84a, 98, 98a]
  Lady Washington had visited Hawaii in 1791 and made a later visit in 1794.
* *Jackal*—British registry, schooner or cutter, Alexander Stewart, master; arrived late in the year about November, departed

December 1793 for Canton with Capt. William Brown, master. [2, 98a]

1794

Discovery—H.B.M sloop, 350 tons, Capt. George Vancouver; on a voyage of exploration; accompanied by *Chatham*, Puget; arrived January 9, 1794, departed March 14, 1794; Archibald Menzies, surgeon and naturalist. [125, 178, 179]
  Discovery had two previous visits to Hawaii in 1792 and 1793.
Chatham—H.B.M. armed tender, 135 tons, Lieut. Peter Puget; accompanied *Discovery*, Vancouver; arrived January 9, 1794, departed March 14, 1794. Edward Bell, clerk, Thomas Manby, master's mate aboard. [18a, 116a, 178, 179]
  Chatham had made two previous visits to Hawaii in 1792 and 1793.
Daedalus—British naval store ship, Lieut. Hergest, under Vancouver; arrived January 9, 1794, departed February 8, 1794. [179]
* *Britannia*—first vessel built in Hawaii, constructed under Vancouver's supervision in February 1794. [2, 125, 178, 179]
* *Jefferson*—American registry, ship, Capt. Josiah Roberts, master; arrived October 1794, departed _____. [84, 84a]
  Jefferson had come before in 1793.
* *Phoenix*—_____ registry, Capt. Hugh Moore, master; arrived September 1794, departed _____ 1794. [84, 84a]
* *Jackal*—English registry, schooner, trader, William Brown, master; arrived November 21, 1794, departed after January 12, 1795. A wad shot in celebration of a native victory from the *Jackal* in Honolulu harbor killed John Kendrick, master of the *Lady Washington*. Later William Brown, involved in intrigue, was killed by the natives. [2, 98a]
* *Prince Lee Boo*—English registry, sloop, trader, Capt. Gordon, master; arrived _____ 1794, departed _____ 1794. Gordon and William Brown, master of the *Jackal*, became involved in intrigue and were killed by the natives. [2, 98a]
* *Lady Washington*—American registry, sloop, Capt. John Kendrick, master; arrived December 3, 1794, departed December

1794. Death of Kendrick in Honolulu harbor caused by wad shot from *Jackal* fired in celebration of a native victory. [1, 98a]

Lady Washington had visited Hawaii in 1791 and 1793.

1795

Union—Boston registry, sloop, 89 tons, John Boit, Jr., master; arrived October 13, 1795, departed October 16, 1795. [25]

Jane—British registry, 100 tons, _____, master; on trading voyage to northwest coast of America; arrived October 13, 1795, departed November 12, 1795. John Myers shipped on her. [134]

* *Ruby*—"of Bristol, England," 101 tons, Charles Bishop, master; arrived _____ 1795, departed _____. [84, 84a]

* *Mercury*—"of New Providence," Capt. Barnett, master; arrived _____ 1795, departed _____ 1795. [84, 84a]

1796

Providence—H.B.M. sloop of war, 400 tons, Capt. William Robert Broughton; on a voyage of discovery; first visit—arrived January 1, 1796, departed February 20, 1796; second visit—arrived July 6, 1796, departed July 31, 1796. [28]

Providence was accompanied by a tender.

* *Arthur*—"from Bengal," snow, trader, Henry Barber, master. In October of 1796, the *Arthur* was wrecked off a point on Oahu now known as "Barber's Point." [1]

Otter—Boston registry, "three masts," Ebenezer Dorr, master; sighted Hawaii December 2, 1796, left Kauai January 1, 1797. Capt. Péron, whose vessel, *Émilie*, had been captured by the English, held position of first officer. [144]

1798

Neptune—American registry, sealing ship, 350 tons, Daniel Greene, master; arrived August 12, 1798, departed August 31, 1798; Ebenezer Townsend, Jr., supercargo. [174]

1799

Eliza—Boston registry, ship, 159 tons, Capt. James Rowan, master; arrived early January 1799, departed "after a few days" for the Northwest Coast. Mr. Burling, clerk of the vessel, probable author of a journal of the voyage. [84c]

Caroline or *Dragon*—American registry, 50 tons, Richard J. Cleveland, master; arrived July 19, 1799, departed July 21, 1799. [35, 36, 84d]

Hancock—"of Boston," trader, Capt. Crocker, master; arrived October 6, 1799, departed October 8–9, 1799. [84d]

1800

* *Alert*—American registry, "of Boston," Capt. William Bowles, master; John Ebbets, first mate; probably in Hawaii in summer of 1800 as she arrived in Canton, China, September 15, 1800. [84a, 84e]

Betsy—British registry, a privateer, ———, master; arrived October 21, 1800, departed October 28, 1800. John Myers was the third officer. [134]

1801

Perseverance—American registry, 200 tons, Amasa Delano, master; arrived December 10, 1801, departed December 20, 1801. [51]

  Perseverance came again in 1806.

1802

Atahualpa—Boston registry, trader, 210 tons, Capt. Dixey Wildes, master; arrived August 5, 1802, departed November 4, 1802. [11, 65, 84b]

  Atahualpa made other visits in 1805, 1812, 1813.

* *Alert*—American registry, "of Boston," John Ebbets, master; probably in Hawaii in fall of 1802 as she arrived in Canton, China, December 8, 1802. [84a, 84e]

Margaret—British registry, ship, John Buyers, master; arrived

9

December 17, 1802, departed January 21, 1803. John Turnbull in charge of cargo and trade. [176]

Ann—American registry, ———, master, arrived December 25, 1802, departed December 28, 1802. John Myers aboard. [134]

1803

Lelia Byrd—American registry, brig, 175 tons, William Shaler, master; Richard J. Cleveland, supercargo; arrived June 21, 1803, departed July 7, 1803; brought first horse to Hawaii. [35, 36]

   Lelia Byrd came again in 1805.

1804

Nadeshda—"Russian imperial service," ship, 450 tons, Capt. Lieut. Adam John von Krusenstern in command; arrived June 7, 1804, departed June 10, 1804. [97, 101, 110]

Neva—"Russian imperial service," ship, 350 tons, Capt. Lieut. Urey Lisiansky in command under von Krusenstern; arrived June 8, 1804, departed June 20, 1804. [97, 101, 110]

   Neva visited Hawaii in 1809.

1805

Pearl—Boston registry, 200 tons, Capt. John Ebbets, master; arrived February 27, 1805, departed March 12, 1805. [84a, 84c]

   Pearl visited again in 1806, 1808.

Lelia Byrd—American registry, brig, 175 tons, William Shaler, master; arrived August 22, 1805. She leaked badly, so Shaler exchanged her for *Tamana* on September 9, 1805. [35, 36, 160]

   Lelia Byrd visited Hawaii in 1803.

Tamana———— registry, schooner, 45 tons, John Hudson, master; built at Hawaii 1805. William Shaler exchanged *Lelia Byrd* for her, September 9, 1805. [35, 36, 160]

Atahualpa—Boston registry, trader, 210 tons, Capt. Adams, master; arrived August 1805, departed October 6, 1805. William Shaler left Hawaii on her. [84b, 160]

   Atahualpa made other visits to Hawaii in 1802 and 1813.

Yarmouth———— registry, snow, ———, master; arrived December 8, 1805, Samuel Patterson on her; departed December 22, 1805. [141] This vessel had been secured at Sitka from the Russians as part payment for the *Juno.* Bancroft calls her the sloop *Ermak.* [9]

1806

*Hamilton—*Boston registry, Capt. Porter, master; arrived ———, departed "early in February" 1806. Samuel Patterson left on her. [141]

*Pearl—*Boston registry, 200 tons, Capt. John Ebbets, master; arrived September 3, 1806 with Samuel Patterson a passenger; departed September 28 to 30, 1806 for Canton. [84a, 84e, 141]
> *Pearl* made other visits, one in 1805.

*Perseverance—*American registry, 200 tons, Amasa Delano, master; arrived September 8, 1806, departed September 30, 1806. [51]
> *Perseverance* came previously in 1801.

Port au Prince—"Private ship of war, belonging to Mr. Robert Bent, of London," 500 tons, Mr. Brown, master; arrived September 29, 1806, departed October 26, 1806; William Mariner, a clerk. [117]

*O'Cain—*Boston registry, 280 tons, in fur trade, Jonathan Winship, master; arrived about September, left about October. Samuel Patterson shipped on her. [9, 84a, 141, 144a, 149a]
> This vessel was a frequent visitor to Hawaii.

Tamana———— registry, schooner, 45 tons, John Hudson, master; arrived ——— 1806, departed ——— 1806. Samuel Patterson arrived on her. [141] *Tamana* had been built at Hawaii in 1805. [35, 36, 160]

1807

Maryland—"from New York," ship, Jonathan Perry, Jr., master, a trader; arrived May 19, 1807, departed July 19, 1807. Isaac Iselin, supercargo; Samuel Patterson, an outbound passenger. [89, 141]

1808

Pearl—Boston registry, 200 tons, Capt. John Suter, master; dates
not known, but on January 9, 1808 she was 334 miles from
the Hawaiian Islands on her way to the northwest coast of
America. [84a]
Pearl had visited in 1805 and 1806.

1809

Neva—"Russian imperial service," ship, 350 tons, Capt. Harge-
meister; arrived January 27, 1809, Archibald Campbell, an
inbound passenger; departed in "three months." [30]
Neva visited Hawaii in 1804, as one of von Krusenstern's
vessels.
Dromo—American registry, trader, 600 tons, Capt. W———, master; arrived February 24, 1809, departed March 15, 1809;
George Little, a seaman. [111]

1810

Duke of Portland—"South-Sea whaler, bound for England," Capt.
Spence, master; arrived February 1810, departed March 4,
1810 with Archibald Campbell an outbound passenger. [30]
* *Albatross*—American registry, ship. Under various masters, she
was an important figure in early trade, approximately 1810–
1816. See *Papers of Hawaiian Historical Society No.* 8 for a
brief review of her career.

1811

Tonquin—American registry, ship, 300 tons, Capt. Jonathan
Thorn, master; arrived February 13, 1811, departed February
28, 1811. John Jacob Astor's first vessel; Alexander Ross and
Gabriel Franchere, clerks. [69, 69a, 154]
New Hazard—Salem registry, brig, 281 tons, trader, Capt. David
Nye, Jr., master; arrived February 27, 1811, departed March
7–8, 1811 for Northwest Coast. Returned for supplies and
sailors September 28, 1811, departed October 15, 1811.

Stephen Reynolds, seaman, aboard. [149a]
New Hazard returned in 1812 and 1813.

Enterprise—American ship "of New York," 291 tons, general trader owned by John Jacob Astor, Capt. John Ebbets, master; arrived September 27, 1811, departed October 15, 1811 for Macao. [84a, 84e]

Enterprise made several trips to Hawaii 1816–1818.

1812

Atahualpa—Boston registry, 210 tons, trader, Capt. John Suter, master; arrived February 26, 1812, departed March 14, 1812. [84a, 84b]

Atahualpa made other visits in 1802, 1805, 1813.

Beaver—American registry, 480 tons, Capt. Cornelius Sowles, master; arrived March 26, 1812, departed April 6, 1812; John Jacob Astor's second vessel; Ross Cox, clerk. [47]

Isabella—Boston-owned, trader, 209 tons, Capt. William Heath Davis, master; dates uncertain but she was already in Hawaii collecting sandalwood when the New Hazard arrived on October 23, 1812, and she was found at anchor in Canton, China, by the New Hazard on February 15, 1813. [84a, 144a, 149a]

New Hazard—Salem registry, brig, 281 tons, trader, Capt. David Nye, Jr., master; arrived October 23, 1812, departed November 13, 1812 for Canton. Stephen Reynolds, seaman aboard. [149a] *See also* 1811 and 1813.

1813

* *Lark*—American registry, _____, Capt. Northcop, master, 1813; John Jacob Astor's third vessel; was wrecked off Kahoolawe. [88]

Isabella—Boston-owned, trader, 209 tons, Capt. William Heath Davis, master; with New Hazard and O'Cain, arrived June 29, 1813, Stephen Reynolds, seaman off New Hazard, aboard. Isabella remained in Hawaii collecting sandalwood until late 1814. [84a, 149a]

Isabella had been in Hawaii in 1812 and returned in 1815.

13

O'Cain—Boston registry, 280 tons, trader, Capt. Jonathan Winship, master; arrived June 29, 1813 and remained to collect sandalwood. [84a, 149a] *See also* 1806.

New Hazard—Salem registry, brig, 281 tons, trader, Capt. David Nye, Jr., master; with *O'Cain* and *Isabella*, arrived June 29, 1813, departed July 26–27, 1813. [149a]

   New Hazard made earlier visits in 1811 and 1812.

Atahualpa—Boston registry, 210 tons, trader, Capt. John Suter, master; arrived October 15, 1813. Sold to a group of Americans who in turn in late 1813 sold the vessel to the Russians, who changed the ship's name to *Bering*. [84b, 144a]

   Atahualpa had made other visits in 1802, 1805, 1812.

1814

Raccoon—British sloop of war, Capt. William Black, master; arrived May 17, 1814, departed May 23, 1814. [86a]

Sir Andrew Hammond—U.S. ship of war, commanded by Lieut. John Gamble of Marine Corps; arrived May 23, 1814, departed June 11, 1814; a British letter of marque ship but captured by the Americans, consequently first war vessel flying U.S. flag to enter Honolulu harbor; retaken by the British ship *Cherub* on June 13; returned to Honolulu June 15–22, 1814. Lieut. Gamble left as a prisoner of war on the *Cherub*, July 16, 1814. [146] *See also* "John M. Gamble" by Edwin North McClellan in *Thirty-fifth Annual Report of The Hawaiian Historical Society for the Year 1926*.

Cherub—British ship of war, Capt. Tucker; arrived June 22, 1814, departed July 16, 1814, with Lieut. John Gamble of *Sir Andrew Hammond* a prisoner of war. [146]

Bering—formerly *Atahualpa*, purchased by the Russians late 1813 who changed name to *Bering*. Arrived October 1814, Capt. James Bennett, master; wrecked off the coast of Kauai during the attempted Russian occupation of that island under Dr. Georg Anton Scheffer, January 31, 1815. [84a, 84b, 144a]

   As the *Atahualpa*, this vessel made earlier visits in 1802, 1805, 1813.

* *Isabella, Othrytie (Discovery), Kodiak (Myrtle), Ilmen,* and

Bering (Atahualpa)—All these were vessels used by the Russians in their attempted occupation, principally on Kauai, led by Dr. Scheffer, 1814–1816. For a discussion of this episode, *see* "The Proceedings of the Russians on Kauai, 1814–1816," in *Papers of the Hawaiian Historical Society No. 6.*

1815

Columbia—British registry, schooner, 185 tons, trader, Anthony Robson, master; arrived January 16, 1815, departed January 18, 1815; Peter Corney, chief officer. [46]
  Columbia made three other visits.
Isabella—Boston-owned ship, trader, 209 tons, Capt. Tyler, master; arrived early November 1815 with Dr. Georg Anton Scheffer a passenger. [144a]
Millwood—"from New York," ship, Samuel G. Bailey, master; arrived December 7, 1815, departed February 16, 1816; Charles H. Barnard on board. [12]
Columbia—British registry, schooner, 185 tons, Capt. Jennings, master; arrived December 10, 1815, departed January 4, 1816; Peter Corney, chief officer. [46]
  Columbia made three other visits.

1816

Ophelia—American registry, ship, about 360 tons, Samuel Hill, master and supercargo; arrived March 28, 1816, departed May 7, 1816. [80a]
Enterprise—American ship "of New York," 291 tons, general trader owned by John Jacob Astor, Capt. John Ebbets, master; arrived June 1816, departed before December 1816. [84a, 84e]
  Enterprise made several trips to Hawaii, 1816–1818.
Rurick—Russian Imperial Navy brig, 180 tons, Lieut. Otto von Kotzebue in command, Louis Choris, artist, and Adelbert von Chamisso, naturalist; arrived November 21, 1816, departed December 14, 1816. [30a, 33, 94, 95]
  Rurick returned in 1817.

1817

Columbia—British registry, schooner, 185 tons, Capt. Jennings, master; arrived January 27, 1817, departed April 16, 1817; Peter Corney, chief officer. [46]

    Columbia made three other visits.

Panther—American brig, 429 tons, Capt. Isaiah Lewis, master; arrived July 4, 1817, departed July 7, 1817 for Macao; Dr. Georg Anton Scheffer aboard. [144a]

Bordeaux Packet—American registry, brig, Andrew Blanchard, master; arrived August 12, 1817, James Hunnewell's first visit; sold to Kalaimoku in December 1817. [85]

Rurick—Russian Imperial Navy brig, 180 tons, Lieut. Otto von Kotzebue in command, Louis Choris, artist, and Adelbert von Chamisso, naturalist; arrived September 27, 1817, departed October 14, 1817. [30a, 33, 94, 95, 144a]

    Rurick had visited Hawaii in 1816.

Columbia—British registry, schooner, 185 tons, Capt Jennings, master; arrived December 6, 1817; Peter Corney, chief officer; sold to Kamehameha I, May 2, 1818. [46]

    Columbia had made three previous visits.

1818

Santa Rosa—"American built, about 300 tons." A pirate ship under Capt. Turner, she arrived in May 1818; bought by Kamehameha I but seized by *Argentina*, Bouchard, late in September 1818; departed October 20, 1818 with Peter Corney in command. [46]

Osprey—"ship, Brown, of Salem, from a sealing voyage"; arrived August 28, 1818, departed September 20, 1818 with James Hunnewell, a passenger. [85]

Argentina—"mounted forty-four guns"; belonged to Independents of South America; commanded by Capt. Hippolyte Bouchard; arrived "end of September" 1818, seized *Santa Rosa*, departed October 20, 1818. For full account of this episode, *see* Peter Corney's book. [46] Probably the same *Argentina* "arrived end of summer 1818" reported by Melvin. [124]

Kamchatka—Russian sloop of war, Capt. Golovnin in command; arrived October 20, 1818, departed after October 30, 1818. [74b, 75]

* *Mentor*—"American ship of Boston," trader, John Suter, master; dates uncertain, but on November 6, 1818, *Mentor* was at the Hawaiian Islands "from the N.W. Coast for Canton." [84a]

1819

Bordelais—French registry, "a three-masted vessel of 200 tons," M. Camille de Roquefeuil, master; arrived January 9, 1819, departed January 26, 1819, on a trading voyage to China. [151]

Uranie—French registry, corvette, Capt. Louis de Freycinet in command of French exploring and scientific expedition; arrived August 8, 1819, departed August 30, 1819. Jacques Arago, draftsman, and Madame de Freycinet aboard. [4, 5, 6, 7, 70a, 70b]

Sylph—_____ registry, brig, Capt. Alexander Adams, master; arrived Hilo November 17, 1819 from Kamchatka, departed _____. Peter Dobell, owner, aboard with wife and child. [53a]

* *Balena*—New Bedford registry, Capt. Edmund Gardner, with *Equator*, first whaleship to visit Hawaiian Islands; in fall of 1819, while at anchor in Kealakekua Bay, caught a whale which yielded 110 barrels of oil; see *The Sailor's Magazine and Naval Journal*, August 1834.

* *Equator*—Nantucket registry, Capt. Elisha Folger, with *Balena*.

1820

Thaddeus—American registry, brig, Capt. Andrew Blanchard, master; arrived at Kailua, Hawaii, April 4, 1820 with pioneer company of American missionaries; departed _____. [81a, 112, 129, 155a, 172]

* *Cleopatra's Barge*—yacht of 191½ tons purchased by Kamehameha II in November 1820 for $90,000, to be paid for in sandalwood; renamed *Haaheo o Hawaii*, meaning *Pride of*

Hawaii. For story, see *Papers of the Hawaiian Historical Society No. 13.*

* *Maro*—Nantucket registry, Joseph Allen, master; first whaleship to enter Honolulu harbor. *See* Thrum's *Hawaiian Annual* for 1909, p. 133.

1821

* *Mentor*—"American ship of Boston," trader, Lemuel Porter, master and one of the owners; arrived late September 1821, departed October 2, 1821. [81a, 84a]

   Mentor had visited Hawaii in 1818 and is mentioned in several accounts as having made visits after 1821.

1822

Mermaid—British registry, sloop, 61 tons, Capt. Kent, master; arrived March 29, 1822, Rev. William Ellis, Daniel Tyerman, and George Bennet, British missionaries, on board; accompanied by *Prince Regent*, departed ———. [61, 177]

   Mermaid returned later in the year.

. *Prince Regent*—schooner, 70 tons; built at Port Jackson, New South Wales; arrived April ——— 1822; convoyed by the *Mermaid*; presented to Kamehameha II on May 1, 1822 as a gift from King of England to fulfill a promise made to Kamehameha I by Vancouver. [60, 61, 177]

America—American registry, ship, ———, master; arrived June 24, 1822, departed August 10, 1822, with Gilbert Farquhar Mathison, a passenger. [119]

Mermaid—British registry, sloop, 61 tons, Capt. Kent, master; arrived July 29, 1822, departed August 22, 1822 with Rev. William Ellis, Daniel Tyerman, and George Bennet, British missionaries, on board. [61, 177]

   Mermaid had visited Hawaii earlier in 1822.

Arrow—"owned by London merchants," Capt. Campbell, master; visited Hawaii during 1822; James Morris, clerk. [182]   The year 1822 is an arbitrary date, chosen after careful reading of the text.

1823

Active——— registry, small schooner, Richard Charlton, master; arrived February 5, 1823, with Rev. William Ellis on his second visit; departed ———. [60]
    Active came again in 1825.

Belgrano—Peruvian brig of war, ———, commander; arrived in latter part of February 1823, John L. Melvin on board; departed ———. [124]

Thames—American registry, ship, Capt. Clasby, master; arrived April 27, 1823 with second company of American missionaries, departed ———. [168]

Foster—Nantucket registry, ship, ———, master; arrived ———, departed in April 1823, returned "end of October" 1823; John L. Melvin on the cruise. [124]

Globe—Nantucket registry, whaleship, Thomas Worth, master; arrived May 1, 1823 and left in few days for Japan; after several months' cruise again touched at Hawaii. Shortly afterwards, the crew mutinied and the survivors, William Lay and Cyrus Hussey, were rescued by the *Dolphin*. [107, 142]

Paragon—American registry, ship, William Cole, master; arrived August 1, 1823, departed February ——, 1824; Charles Brewer's first visit. [27]   John L. Melvin [124] speaks of leaving on the *Paragon* in November 1823, presumably the same vessel on which Brewer came.

* *Aigle*—British registry, whaler, Capt. Valentine Starbuck, master; arrived ———, departed November 27, 1823 with Kamehameha II and suite, passengers for England. [1, 129]

1824

Russell—American registry, ship, Capt. Coleman, master; arrived ———, departed September ——, 1824, with Rev. William Ellis a free passenger. [60, 61, 129]

Tamaahmaah—American, brig, 240 tons, trader, Capt. John Meek, master; arrived August 9, 1824, departed November 13, 1824 for Sitka. George Barrell, seaman, aboard. [12a]

Predpriatie—Russian Imperial Navy frigate, Post Capt. Otto von

Kotzebue in command; arrived December 13, 1824, departed January 31, 1825. [96]

Predpriatie returned later in 1825.

1825

Ontario—American registry, whaling ship, Alex. D. Bunker, master; arrived April 3, 1825, departed April 8, 1825. [29]

Ontario returned twice in 1826.

* *Active*—_____ registry, "small schooner," _____, master; arrived April 16, 1825, with Richard Charlton, British consul at Honolulu, on board; departed _____. [1, 129]

Active had come in 1823.

Blonde—British Royal Navy frigate, Capt. George Anson Byron (or Lord Byron) in command, Robert Dampier, artist and draftsman, Andrew Bloxam, naturalist, and James Macrae, botanist; arrived May 3, 1825, departed July 18, 1825. *Blonde* brought back the bodies of Kamehameha II and Kamamalu who had died of measles in London. [22, 47a, 76, 116]

Tartar—American registry, schooner, 154 tons, in fur trade, Capt. Benjamin Morrell, Jr., master; arrived June 22, 1825, departed June 29, 1825. [130]

Predpriatie—Russian Imperial Navy frigate, Post Capt. Otto von Kotzebue in command; arrived September 12, 1825, departed September 19, 1825. [96]

Predpriatie had visited Hawaii in December of 1824.

* *Daniel*—British registry, whaleship, Capt. Buckle, master. During October 1825 sailors from this ship attacked Mr. Richards' house at Lahaina. The incident sometimes is called "the first Lahaina outrage." [1, 129]

Fawn—British registry, ship, Capt. Dale, master; arrived _____, departed October 17, 1825 with C. S. Stewart a passenger. [168]

Stanton—American registry, whaler, Capt. Howland, master, October 1825. [1, 52] Reuben Delano, seaman, mentions *Daniel* at Lahaina and the outrage committed by her sailors, so *Stanton*'s date must be October 1825.

1826

Dolphin—U.S. schooner, Lieut. John Percival in command; arrived January 16, 1826, departed May 11, 1826. [142] Wm. Lay and Cyrus Hussey, survivors of the *Globe* mutiny, were on board. [107] The conduct of Percival and his men resulted in an investigation by a Naval Court of Inquiry which exonerated Percival.

Stanton—American registry, whaler, Capt. Howland, master; arrived February 1826; departed _____. [20, 52] Reuben Delano mentions a missionary house pulled down by sailors. Probably this is an incorrect version of the outrage by *Dolphin*'s crew referred to by Hiram Bingham. [20]

Ontario—American registry, whaling ship, Alex. D. Bunker, master; arrived March 8, 1826, departed April 16, 1826. [29]
     Ontario had visited Hawaii in 1825. She returned again in September 1826.

Rosellic—American registry, whaler, Capt. Gardner, master; arrived in March 1826, departed _____; came again in the fall of the same year; William Nevens, ship keeper. [135]
     Rosellic returned in 1827.

Blossom—H.B.M. sloop, Capt. Frederick William Beechey in command; arrived May 20, 1826, departed June 1, 1826 on a voyage of exploration in the north Pacific. [16, 148]
     Blossom returned in 1827.

Ontario—American registry, whaling ship, Alex. D. Bunker, master; arrived September 1, 1826, departed September 25, 1826. [29]
     Ontario had visited Hawaii in 1825 and again in March of 1826.

Missionary Packet—American registry, 40 tons, James Hunnewell, master; arrived October 21, 1826; intended for use between islands by American missionaries but subsequently sold. [86]

* *Peacock*—U.S. sloop of war, Capt. Thomas ap Catesby Jones in command; arrived in October 1826, stayed three months. Jones settled American claims and generally produced a better feeling between the United States and Hawaii. [98a]

* *Several whalers* at Lahaina—During October of 1826, the crews

21

from certain vessels had a riot on shore, sometimes called "the second Lahaina outrage." The names and masters of these boats are not given in Alexander's *History* or *The Missionary Herald*. [1, 129]

* *Wellington*—ship from San Blas, Mexico, ———, master; introduction of mosquitoes at Lahaina, 1826. [1]

1827

Blossom—H.B.M. sloop, Capt. Frederick William Beechey in command; arrived January 26, 1827, from a voyage of exploration in the north Pacific, departed March 4, 1827. [16, 148]

    Blossom had visited Hawaii in 1826.

Rosellic—American registry, whaler, Capt. Gardner, master; arrived in March 1827, returned again in September 1827; William Nevens, ship keeper. [135]

    Rosellic had visited Hawaii in 1826.

* *Comet*—French registry, ship, Capt. Plassard, master; arrived July 7, 1827 with first Catholic missionaries on board, departed ———. [1]

* *John Palmer*—British registry, whaler, Capt. Elisha Clarke, master; during October 1827, sailors from this vessel made an assault at Lahaina, sometimes referred to as "the third Lahaina outrage." [1]

Owhyhee—Boston registry, brig, 116 (166?) tons, trader, left Honolulu for Boston via Canton, late 1827. George Barrell, seaman off *Tamaahmaah*, aboard. [12a]

1828

Parthian—American registry, merchant ship, 337 tons, Capt. Richard D. Blinn, master; arrived March 31, 1828 with third company of American missionaries, departed ———. [78, 91, 92]

Alzire—French registry, brig, Capt. Darluc; sighted Mauna Loa April 28, 1828, departed ———; Gabriel Lafond on board. [99]

Heros—French registry, commercial vessel, 370 tons, Capt. Abel

Duhaut-Cilly, master; arrived September 17, 1828, departed November 15, 1828. Edmond LeNetrel, officer, aboard. [57, 109a]

Wilhelmina en Maria—Dutch registry, ship, in command of _____; arrived in 1828. Jacobus Boelen's book is in Dutch and no translation has been found. [23]

1829

Volunteer—Boston-owned bark, Capt. Charles Taylor, master; arrived January 28, departed February 13, 1829, with Jonathan S. Green, American missionary, a passenger for the Northwest Coast, sent to report on a possible new field in which the American Board might open a new mission. *Volunteer*, with Green aboard, returned November 9, 1829. [77]

Vincennes—U.S. naval corvette, Capt. William Finch in command; arrived October 2, 1829, departed November 24, 1829; Charles S. Stewart, the chaplain. [169]

Canton—American registry, whaler, Capt. Abraham Gardner, master; arrived fall of 1829, departed _____. John Slade, a seaman [164], mentions the *Vincennes*.

  Canton came again in 1830.

* *Kamehameha*—Hawaiian registry, brig, with *Becket* made ill-fated expedition to the south in search of sandalwood under Boki's leadership; departed December 2, 1829 and was lost mysteriously with all on board. [1, 98, 98a]

* *Becket*—Hawaiian registry, with *Kamehameha* made ill-fated expedition in search of sandalwood under Boki's leadership; departed December 2, 1829, returned August 3, 1830, with news of disaster. [1, 98, 98a]

1830

Glide—American registry, Capt. Henry Archer, master; arrived October 9, 1830, departed October 15, 1830; James Oliver, a seaman. [137]

Canton—American registry, whaler, Capt. Abraham Gardner, master; arrived _____ 1830; departed _____. John Slade, seaman, left the boat here. [164]

  Canton had come in 1829 also.

Harriet Blanchard—_____ registry, schooner, Capt. Levi Young, master; arrived _____, departed during 1830 with John Slade on board. [164]

1831

Kent—British registry, whaler; Capt. _____; arrived May 5, 1831, departed "end of month" 1831; Thomas Beale, ship's surgeon. [15]

* *New England*—"from New Bedford," ship, Capt. Parker, master; arrived June 7, 1831 with fourth company of American missionaries, departed _____. [129]

Princess Louise—Prussian registry, Capt. Wendt in command; third Prussian voyage around the world; arrived June 24, 1831, departed _____. Dr. F. J. F. Meyen, physician and naturalist, on board. [126, 127]

* *Waverly*—_____ registry, brig, Capt. Sumner, master; arrived _____, departed December 24, 1831 with the banished Catholic missionaries. [1]

Baltic—Nantucket registry, whaleship, Capt. Chadwick, master; visited Hawaii for two weeks during 1831; George A. Dodge, seaman. [54]

1832

Chinchilla—American registry, brig, Capt. _____ Meek, master; arrived during April 1832 with James Oliver on board, departed _____. [137]

Averick—American registry, whaleship, Capt. Edward Swain, master; arrived May 17, 1832 with fifth company of American missionaries, departed _____. [31, 63, 115a]

Potomac—U.S.N. frigate, Commodore John Downes in command; arrived July 23, 1832, departed August 16, 1832. James Oliver, seaman, J. N. Reynolds, private secretary to Downes, Francis Warriner, school master. [137, 149, 186]

Sarah and Elizabeth—British registry, whaler, Capt. Swain, master; arrived August 30, 1832, departed September 11, 1832; Thomas Beale, ship's surgeon. [15]

————arrived August ——, 1832, departed ———. David Douglas, the eminent Scottish botanist, came by this boat on his first visit to these islands. [55, 56]

Japan—British ship employed in sperm whale fishery, Capt. John May, master; sighted Hawaii October 29, 1832, departed December 3, 1832. [89a]

1833

Huntress—American registry, whaler, Capt. Post, master; arrived April 1, 1833, departed ———; William Torrey, seaman. [173]

 Huntress came again in 1834.

* *Mentor*—"from New London," ship, Capt. Rice, master; arrived May 1, 1833 with sixth company of American missionaries, departed ———. [129]

————arrived December 23, 1833, departed ———. David Douglas, the eminent Scottish botanist, returned by this ship for his second visit to these islands. The following July he was killed on the island of Hawaii. A tablet to his memory has been placed on the exterior of Kawaiahao church in Honolulu. [55, 56]

1834

Tuscan—British registry, whaleship, 300 tons, T. R. Stavers, master; arrived April 16, 1834, departed May 22, 1834; F. D. Bennett, zoologist, on board. [19]

 Tuscan returned in October of 1834 and again in October of 1835.

Huntress—American registry, whaler, Capt. Post, master; arrived October 1, 1834, departed October 15, 1834; William Torrey, seaman. [173]

 Huntress had visited Hawaii in 1833.

Tuscan—British registry, whaleship, 300 tons, T. R. Stavers, master; arrived October 2, 1834, departed October 20, 1834; F. D. Bennett, zoologist, on board. [19]

 Tuscan had visited here in April of 1834. She came again in October 1835.

1835

Mary Dacre—_____ registry, brig, Capt. Lambert, master; arrived
January 5, 1835, departed March 26, 1835; John K. Townsend
a passenger from and for Oregon. [175]

Hobomok—American registry, whaler, Capt. Barnard, master;
arrived March 25, 1835, departed April 29, 1835; William
Nevens, ship keeper. [135]

* *Hellespont*—"from Boston," ship, Capt. Henry, master; arrived
June 6, 1835 with seventh company of American missionaries,
departed _____. [129]

Tuscan—British registry, whaleship, 300 tons, T. R. Stavers, master; arrived October 4, 1835, departed November 4, 1835;
F. D. Bennett, zoologist, on board. [19]
    Tuscan had come twice in 1834.

Ganymede—bark, owned by Hudson Bay Co., Capt. Eales, master;
arrived November 1835 with Daniel Lee, a passenger from
Oregon; departed _____. [109]

Henry Freeling—British registry, 101 tons, Capt. Keen, master;
arrived December 26, 1835, departed June 29, 1836; Daniel
Wheeler, a minister of the Society of Friends, on board. [187]

1836

Chelsea—American registry, clipper ship, whaler, Capt. B_____,
master; arrived March 22, 1836, departed April 26, 1836.
William M. Davis, a seaman [50], mentions Daniel Wheeler,
so the year must have been 1836. [187]

Columbia—British registry, Hudson Bay Co.'s bark, Capt. Darby,
master; arrived July 14, 1836 with Rev. Samuel Parker a
passenger, departed August 1, 1836. [140, 158]

Nereid—bark, owned by Hudson Bay Co., Capt. Royal, master;
arrived _____, departed August 1836 with Daniel Lee a passenger for Oregon. [109]

Enterprise—U.S.N. schooner, Capt. George N. Hollins in command under Commodore Kennedy; arrived September 6,
1836, departed September 26, 1836. [156, 158]
    Enterprise with *Peacock* constituted the East India and
Asiatic squadron.

Peacock—U.S.N. ship, 600 tons, Commodore Edmund P. Kennedy in command; arrived September 7, 1836, departed October 9, 1836; Dr. W. S. W. Ruschenberger, surgeon. [156, 158]
   Peacock with *Enterprise* constituted the East India and Asiatic squadron.

Bonite—French naval corvette, 800 tons, Capt. Auguste Nicolas Vaillant in command, on a government expedition; arrived September 28, 1836, departed October 24, 1836. Barthelme Lauvergne and Théodore Auguste Fisquet, artists with the expedition. [13, 106, 181a]   Vaillant obtained permission for the Irish Catholic priest, Robert Walsh, who arrived on the *Garafilia*, to remain in Hawaii.

* *Garafilia*—American registry, brig, Seymour, master; arrived September 30, 1836, departed October 11, 1836. [1, 158] Brought Robert Walsh, Irish Catholic priest, who, because he was a British subject, was allowed to remain provided he did not teach the Hawaiians. Capt Vaillant of the *Bonite* obtained this permission for Walsh.

* *Acteon*—British sloop of war, Lord Edward Russell in command; arrived October 23, 1836, departed November 19, 1836. [1, 158]   On November 16, Lord Russell negotiated a treaty between Great Britain and the Sandwich Islands which defined the rights of British subjects.

Phoenix—"from New London," ship, 410 tons, Capt. Allyn, master; arrived November 4, 1836, departed December 17, 1836 with Rev. Samuel Parker a passenger. [140, 158]

Columbia—British registry, Hudson Bay Co.'s bark, 300 tons, Capt. Royal, master; arrived December 23, 1836 with John K. Townsend a passenger from Oregon; departed January 5, 1837. [158, 175]

Hamilton—American registry, ship, Capt. S. Barker, master; arrived December 23, 1836 with Dr. Elijah White a passenger; left January 23, 1836. [2, 158]

1837

Europa—American registry, ship, Capt. Shaw, master; arrived January 19, 1837, departed March 16, 1837 with John K. Townsend a passenger for Valparaiso. [175]

The Boy—American registry, whaler, 260 tons, Capt. Barton, master; arrived March 1, 1837, departed _____; returned _____; William Nevens, ship keeper. [135]

Diana—American registry, brig, Capt. Hinckley, master; arrived _____, left April 8, 1837 with Dr. Elijah White an outbound passenger. [2, 158]

Mary Frazier—Boston registry, bark, 288 tons, Capt. Charles Sumner, master; arrived April 9, 1837 with eighth company of American missionaries; departed for Manila April 26, 1837. [129, 158, 188a]

California—Mexican registry, schooner, 18 tons, Falkland (Faughlan) owner and master; arrived April 16, 1837, left May 6, 1837; James Jenkins, supercargo. [90, 158]

* *Clementine*—British registry, brig, Capt. Handley, master; arrived April 17, 1837 with Catholic missionaries Bachelot and Short. [1, 98, 98a, 145, 158]

Sulphur—H.B.M. ship, 380 tons, Capt. Sir Edward Belcher in command, Richard Brinsley Hinds, surgeon; arrived July 8, 1837, departed July 27, 1837. With Du Petit-Thouars on the *Venus*, Belcher became involved in the trouble over the return of the Catholic priests on the *Clementine*. [17, 80b]
   Sulphur returned in 1839.

Starling—H.B.M. schooner, tender to *Sulphur*, Lieut. Henry Kellett in command under Capt. Edward Belcher; arrived July 10, 1837, departed July 27, 1837. [17]
   Starling returned in 1839.

Vénus—French naval frigate, Capt. Abel Du Petit-Thouars in command; arrived July 10, 1837, departed July 24, 1837. [58]   With Belcher on the *Sulphur*, Du Petit-Thouars became involved in the troubles over the return of the Catholic priests on the *Clementine*. He signed a treaty assuring for Frenchmen rights equal with other foreigners.

_____–_____ registry, whaler, Capt. Coleman, master; arrived _____, departed August 1, 1837; William Torrey, a seaman. [173]

* *Peru*—American registry, brig, chartered by merchants Peirce and Brewer of Honolulu, Capt. G. E. Kilham, master; arrived July 29, 1837 with James Jackson Jarves as passenger; cruised among the Hawaiian Islands and left under the com-

mand of Capt. Henry A. Peirce, October 30, 1837 with Patrick Short, Catholic missionary as passenger. [89a, 98a, 158]

Imogene—H.M.S. frigate, 26 guns, Capt. Bruce in command; arrived September 29, 1837, departed October 17, 1837; Sir John C. Dalrymple Hay, a midshipman. [79]   Capt. Bruce tried to help in troubles over Catholic priests. He also placed a copper tablet on the stump of a coconut tree at Kealakekua in memory of Capt. Cook.

* Europa—American registry, ship, Capt. Shaw, master; arrived November 2, 1837 with Maigret and Murphy, Catholic missionaries, passengers; departed November 25, 1837. [1, 158]

* Our Lady of Peace—formerly Missionary Packet, schooner, bought by Catholics so Maigret and Bachelot might depart November 23, 1837. [1, 98, 98a]

* Clementine—British registry, brig, owned by Jules Dudoit of Honolulu, Capt. Blinn, master; departed from Hawaii December 5, 1837 with James Jackson Jarves as passenger. [89b, 98a, 154]

1839

* Fama—American registry, ship, Capt. Cornelius Hoyer, master; arrived April 6, 1839 with James Jackson Jarves and wife as passengers. [89b, 154]

Sulphur—H.B.M. ship, 380 tons, Capt. Sir Edward Belcher in command, Richard Brinsley Hinds, surgeon; arrived May 30, 1839, departed June 16, 1839. [17, 80b]
    Sulphur had visited Hawaii in 1837.

Starling—H.B.M. schooner, tender to Sulphur, Lieut. Henry Kellett in command under Capt. Edward Belcher; arrived June 1, 1839, departed June 16, 1839. [17]
    Starling had come in 1837 to Hawaii.

Artémise—French naval frigate, Post Capt. Laplace in command; arrived July 9, 1839, departed July 20, 1839. [105]   Laplace's visit was one of avowed hostility. He forced the Hawaiian government under duress to sign a treaty and to pay $20,000 guaranty.

Ville de Bordeaux—French registry, whaler, _____, master; ar-

29

rived "end of September, 1839," "stayed some weeks"; Dr. Thiercelin on board. [171]

Columbia—U.S. frigate, Commodore George C. Read in command; arrived October 10, 1839, departed November 4, 1839; accompanied by *John Adams,* Capt. Thomas Wyman. J. Henshaw Belcher, an officer [18], William M. Murrell one of crew [133], Fitch W. Taylor, chaplain [170]. Read's visit helped to ease the tension caused by Laplace of the *Artémise.*

John Adams—U.S. sloop, Capt. Thomas Wyman in command, in company with U.S. frigate *Columbia.*

Relief—U.S.N. store ship with Wilkes Exploring Expedition; "sent home from Callao by way of Sandwich Islands and Sydney," Lieut. A. K. Long in command. Arrived September 5, 1839, departed September 19, 1839. [34, 43, 64, 189]

Vancouver—_____ registry, barque, Capt. Duncan, master; arrived December 16, 1839, departed February 22, 1840. Thomas J. Farnham arrived on the *Vancouver.* [66, 67, 98a]

1840

Don Quixote—Hawaiian registry, bark, Capt. Paty, master; arrived February 15, departed March 24, 1840 with Thomas J. Farnham a passenger. [66, 67, 98a]

Lausanne—"from New York," ship, 500 tons, Capt. T. Spaulding, master; arrived April 11, 1840, departed April 28, 1840 with Joseph H. Frost and Rev. Gustavus Hines passengers for Oregon. [81, 109]

* *Clementine*—British registry, brig, Capt. Walker, master; arrived May 15, 1840 with Catholic missionaries Maigret, Rouchouse, and two others. [1, 145]

North America—American registry, bark, whaler, Capt. Richards, master; arrived May 22, 1840 with Francis Allyn Olmsted a passenger, departed _____. [138]

Flora—American registry, bark, merchant vessel, Capt. Spring, master; arrived June 19, departed August 3, 1840 with Francis Allyn Olmsted, Rev. Hiram Bingham, and several others of the American missionary group. [20, 138]

Flying Fish—U.S.N. tender, 96 tons, Commandant Samuel Knox;

arrived September 20, 1840, departed December 2, 1840; Wilkes Exploring Expedition. [34, 43, 64, 189]
   Flying Fish returned in November 1841.
Vincennes—U.S.N. sloop of war, 780 tons, Commodore Charles Wilkes; arrived September 23, 1840, left April 5, 1841; Wilkes Exploring Expedition. [34, 43, 64, 189]
   Vincennes returned in November 1841.
Peacock—U.S.N. sloop of war, 650 tons, Capt. William L. Hudson; arrived September 30, 1840, departed December 2, 1840; wrecked July 18, 1841 at mouth of Columbia River; replaced by *Oregon*, Carr; Wilkes Exploring Expedition. [34, 43, 64, 189]
Porpoise—U.S.N. brig, 230 tons, Lieut. Cadwalader Ringgold; arrived October 8, 1840, departed for a survey of the Paumotus November 15, 1840, returned to Hawaii March 24, 1841 and finally departed April 5, 1841; Wilkes Exploring Expedition. [34, 43, 64, 189]
   Porpoise returned in November 1841.
Maryland—American registry, brig, Capt. Couch, master; arrived October 21, 1840 with Dr. Elijah White a passenger, departed December 22, 1840. [2, 145]
Lausanne—"from New York," ship, 500 tons, Capt. T. Spaulding, master; arrived _____, left December 2, 1840 with Dr. Elijah White a passenger for New England. [2, 145]

1841

India—American registry, whaleship, Capt. Chas. W. Gelett, master; arrived in April 1841, departed _____; arrived October 1841, departed _____. [72]
* *Gloucester*—"from Boston," ship, Capt. Eastabrook, master; arrived May 21, 1841 with ninth company of American missionaries; departed (January 20, 1842?). [129, 145]
Vincennes—U.S.N. sloop of war, 780 tons, Commodore Charles Wilkes; arrived November 17, 1841, departed November 27, 1841; Wilkes Exploring Expedition. [34, 43, 64, 189]
   Vincennes had come in 1840.
Oregon—U.S.N. brig, Lieut. Overton Carr; arrived November 17, 1841, departed November 27, 1841; Wilkes Exploring Expe-

dition. [34, 43, 64, 189]   *Oregon* was purchased to replace *Peacock*, Hudson, 1840.

Flying Fish—U.S.N. tender, 96 tons, Commandant Samuel Knox; arrived November 17, 1841, departed November 27, 1841, Wilkes Exploring Expedition. [34, 43, 64, 189]

   Flying Fish had visited Hawaii in 1840.

Porpoise—U.S.N. brig, Lieut. Cadwalader Ringgold; arrived November 17, 1841, departed November 27, 1841; Wilkes Exploring Expedition. [34, 43, 64, 189]

   Porpoise had visited Hawaii in 1840.

1842

* *Gloucester*—"from Boston," ship, Capt. Eastabrook, master; arrived (May 21, 1841?), departed January 20, 1842 with James Jackson Jarves a passenger. [89b, 145]

Cowlitz—bark owned by Hudson Bay Co., _____, master; arrived February 10, 1842, left March 24, 1842; Sir George Simpson, a passenger. [162]   *Cawlitz* which arrived in July 1842 was probably the same vessel. [26]

_____—French registry, _____, master; arrived June 21, 1842 with J.-B. Z. Bolduc, Catholic missionary to Columbia River; departed _____. [26]

* *Shaw*—_____ registry, schooner, _____, master; arrived _____, departed July 8, 1842. William Richards and Timothy Haalilio, passengers, on embassy to foreign powers. [1, 98]
   The name of this vessel was found in Mr. Richards' diary owned by the Archives of Hawaii.

Cawlitz—British registry, bark, belonged to Hudson Bay Co., _____, master; arrived July 29, 1842, departed August 18, 1842, with J.-B. Z. Bolduc a passenger. [26]   *Cowlitz* which had visited Hawaii in February 1842 was probably the same vessel. [162]

* *Embuscade*—French corvette, Captain Mallet; arrived August 24, 1842, departed _____. Mallet made certain demands but when informed of Hawaiian embassy sent to France to ask for a new treaty, he left without pressing them further. [1, 98, 98a]

* *Maryland*—_____ registry, _____, master; arrived _____, de-

parted September 26, 1842 with Richard Charlton, British consul at Honolulu, a passenger. [1, 98] The name of this vessel was found in a letter by George Pelly owned by the Archives of Hawaii.

* Sarah Abigail—"from Boston," brig, Capt. Doane, master; arrived September 21, 1842 with tenth company of American missionaries, departed ———. [129]

1843

* Carysfort—H.B.M. frigate, Capt. Lord George Paulet; arrived February 10, 1843, departed August 25, 1843.

Provisional cession of Hawaii to Great Britain, February 25, 1843, followed acts of Lord Paulet supporting machinations of Richard Charlton, British consul. Rear Admiral Richard Thomas restored the Hawaiian flag, July 31, 1843. [1, 71, 98, 98a]

* Boston—U.S. ship of war, Commander J. C. Long in command; arrived February 13, 1843, departed March 17, 1843. [1, 71]

* Albert—better known as Hooikaika, schooner about 71 tons belonging to Kamehameha III, seized and renamed by Lord Paulet. Departed on March 11, 1843, with dispatches for British Foreign Office. Passengers—Alexander Simpson, British agent; J. F. B. Marshall, secret envoy of Kamehameha III. For brief account of Hooikaika's history see "Hawaiian Maritime History" in Thrum's Hawaiian Annual for 1890.

* Victoria—Hawaiian schooner belonging to Kamehameha III; seized by Lord Paulet and sent March 17, 1843 to Valparaiso with dispatches for Admiral Thomas. [1, 71]

Wales———— registry, ship, ———, master; arrived May 9, 1843 from New York with Rev. Henry T. Cheever a passenger. Wales departed May 10, 1843 for China. [32]

* Hazard—H.B.M. ship, Capt. Bell; arrived July 2, 1843, departed October 30, 1843. [1, 71]

* Constellation—U.S.N. frigate, Commodore L. Kearney; arrived July 6, 1843, departed August 16 for California. [1, 71]

United States—U.S. frigate, Capt. James Armstrong in command, attached to U.S. Pacific Squadron under Commodore Thomas ap Catesby Jones; arrived Hilo July 23, 1843, departed from

Honolulu August 20, 1843. R. S. Franklin, a midshipman. Herman Melville, famous as author of *Typee* and other books, left on her as a seaman. [2a, 70, 71]

* *Dublin*—H.B.M. flagship, Rear Admiral Richard Thomas; arrived July 26, 1843; restoration of Hawaiian flag July 31, 1843; departed August 11, 1843. [1, 71, 98]

Cyane—U.S. Navy sloop of war, Commander Cornelius K. Stribling in command; arrived August 4, 1843 bringing news of the success of the king's envoys in Europe, departed November 6, 1843 for Monterey. William H. Myers, author and artist, gunner on board. [1, 2a, 71, 127a]

Bhering—Boston registry, bark, Capt. B. F. Snow; arrived September 3, 1843, left November 18, 1843, with Daniel Lee and Joseph H. Frost passengers for Boston. [71, 109]

Diamond—"from England," bark, Capt. Fowler; arrived September 16, 1843 with Daniel Lee and Joseph H. Frost, passengers from Oregon; departed November 25, 1843. [109]

1844

* *Hazard*—H.B.M. ship, Capt. Bell; arrived February 3, 1844 with passengers, William Miller, consul-general for Great Britain, and Robert Crichton Wyllie, secretary of the consul-general and afterwards Minister of Foreign Affairs, 1845–1863; departed March 1, 1844 for Sydney. [1, 71]

Chenamus—American registry, brig, Capt. Couch, master; arrived February 23, 1844, departed April 3, 1844 with Gustavus Hines, a passenger for Oregon. [71, 81]

Columbia—English registry, bark, Capt. Humphries, master; arrived from Oregon February 27, 1844 with Gustavus Hines and John Ricord passengers, departed April 2, 1844. [71, 81]

* *Congaree*—American registry, ship, Capt. Weston, master; arrived April 18, 1844, James Jackson Jarves a passenger. [89b, 145, 158]

* *Globe*—"from Boston," brig, Capt. Doane, master; arrived July 15, 1844 with eleventh company of American missionaries, departed November 20, 1844. [71]

Savannah—U.S.N. ship, Capt. James Armstrong; arrived August

30, 1844, departed October 3, 1844; Wm. M. Wood, surgeon. [71, 192]

    Savannah came again in 1845.

Lewis—New Bedford registry, whaleship, Capt. Tollman, master; arrived September 16, 1844, departed ———. John Cook, ship's carpenter, arrived on her. He made his home in the Hawaiian Islands until his death in 1916. [45]

* *Commodore Preble*—American whaleship from Lynn, Mass., Capt. Ludlow, master; arrived in Honolulu September 25 and departed September 26, 1844 "bound home." Rev. Henry T. Cheever left aboard this vessel. [32, 71]

Uncas—American registry, whaleship, Capt. Chas. W. Gelett, master; touched at Hawaiian Islands several times during the whaling seasons of 1844 and 1845. [72]

    Uncas came again in 1847 and 1848.

1845

* *Montreal*—American registry, ship, Capt. Snow, master; arrived March 23, 1845 with William Richards, passenger, returning from embassy to foreign powers; Timothy Haalilio, the other envoy, died during the long voyage from Boston. [1, 71, 98, 98a]

Steiglitz—American registry, whaleship, Capt. Selah Young, master; arrived April 27, 1845 with Samuel Snow aboard, departed May 4, 1845. [71, 165]

Portsmouth—U.S.N. ship, Commander John B. Montgomery; arrived August 24, 1845, departed September 5, 1845; Wm. M. Wood, ship's surgeon. [71, 192]

Savannah—U.S.N. frigate, Commodore John D. Sloat in command; arrived September 8, 1845, departed October 12, 1845; John M. Kell, a midshipman. [71, 93]

    Savannah came in 1844 also.

Canton—American registry, whaleship, Capt. Dyke, master; arrived September 30, 1845, departed November 12, 1845 with Samuel Snow aboard. [71, 165]

Leland—American registry, merchant ship, T. Kellington, master; arrived October 2, 1845, departed October 15, 1845 with Gustavus Hines a passenger. [71, 81]

Chenamus—American registry, brig, Capt. Sylvester, master; arrived October 3, 1845 with Gustavus Hines a passenger from Oregon, departed ————. [81]

Constitution—U.S. frigate, Capt. John Percival; arrived November 16, 1845, departed December 2, 1845; also known as *Old Ironsides*. Benjamin Stevens, clerk for Percival. [71, 167]

1846

* *Kamehameha III*—American, "schooner yacht," Capt. Fisher Ames Newell, master; arrived March 8, 1846. Purchased by King Kamehameha III. [135a]

* *Virginie*—French naval frigate, Rear Admiral Hamelin; arrived March 22, 1846, departed April 3, 1846. [71]   Rear Admiral Hamelin restored the $20,000 taken by Capt. Laplace in 1839. M. Emile Perrin, French commissioner, brought new treaties. [1, 71]

Mariposa—American registry, merchant ship, 330 tons, Capt. Spalding, master; arrived May 15, 1846 with Chester Smith Lyman a passenger, departed June 2, 1846. [115]

* *Cormorant*—H.B.M. steamer, Capt. Gordon, master; arrived May 22, 1846, departed May 30, 1846. First steamer to visit Hawaii. [71, 145]

Congress—U.S. frigate, Commodore Robert F. Stockton; arrived June 10, 1846 with Anthony Ten Eyck and Joel Turrill, passengers, and Walter Colton, chaplain; departed June 23, 1846. [41, 42, 71, 180]

Collingwood—H.B.M. ship, 80 guns, Rear Admiral Sir George F. Seymour; arrived August 6, 1846, departed September 3, 1846; Lieut. Fred Walpole an officer. [71, 183]

Galathea—Danish naval corvette, 26 guns, Capt. Steen Bille in command; arrived October 5, 1846, departed November 16, 1846. [19a, 71, 152, 153]   On October 16, 1846, Bille negotiated a Danish treaty with Hawaii.

* *Henry*—American registry, brig, Capt. Kilborn, master; arrived October 12, 1846 with passengers, William L. Lee, afterwards Chief Justice of the Supreme Court, and Charles Reed Bishop, founder of the Bank of Bishop and Bishop Museum; departed ————. [1, 71]

1847

Euphemia—Hawaiian registry, brig, Capt. Thomas Russum, master; arrived ———, departed June 5, 1847 with Chester Smith Lyman a passenger. [115]

* *Providence*—French registry, schooner, Mitchell, master; arrived ———, departed August 21, 1847 with John Ricord a passenger for San Francisco. [71]

Uncas—American registry, whaleship, Capt. Chas. W. Gelett, master; touched at Hawaiian Islands several times during the seasons of 1847 and 1848. [72]

Uncas had been a frequent visitor during the seasons of 1844–1845.

1848

* *Sarcelle*—French naval corvette, Le Borgne in command; arrived February 1, 1848 with Patrick Dillon, French consul for Hawaii, a passenger; departed March 4, 1848. [1, 71]

* *Starling*—Hawaiian schooner, Capt. Winckley, master; sailed February 4, 1848 for San Francisco. James Jackson Jarves left Hawaii for the last time aboard the *Starling*. [89b, 145, 158]

* *Samoset*—"from Boston," ship, Capt. Hollis, master; arrived February 26, 1848 with twelfth company of American missionaries, departed March 11, 1848. [71]

Plover—H.B.M. bark, Commander T. E. L. Moore in command; arrived August 23, 1848, departed August 25, 1848, in search of the *Erebus* and *Terror* under Franklin; Lieut. Wm. Hulme Hooper, an officer. [83]

Independence—U.S. ship, Com. Shubrick; arrived Lahaina August 12, 1848, departed Honolulu September 21, 1848; Lieut. Wise an officer. [71, 191]

Tsar—American registry, merchant ship, 700 tons, Samuel Kenneday, master; arrived September 17, 1848; John Whidden, a seaman; departed November 10, 1848. Whidden deserted at Honolulu. [188]

Samuel Robertson—"of Fairhaven," whaleship, Capt. Turner,

master; arrived November 1848, departed November 11–15, 1848. John Whidden, seaman who deserted from *Tsar*, left aboard *Samuel Robertson*. [188]

Josephine—American registry, whaleship, Capt. Hedges, master; arrived December 24, 1848 with S. S. Hill a passenger; departed January 13, 1849. [71, 80]

1849

Mary—"under protectorate flag," i.e., French, bark, Capt. Fleury, master; arrived March 2, 1849, departed March 10, 1849; Edward Lucatt on board. [114]

Massachusetts—U.S. transport, sailing steamer, 750 tons, Capt. Wood, master; arrived April 9, 1849, departed April 17, 1849; carried the first U.S. troops to garrison forts of Oregon. Second steam vessel to visit Hawaii. [169a]

Planet—American registry, whaler, Capt. Peter Smith Buck, master; arrived April 20, 1849, departed _____. Edward T. Perkins, seaman, arrived on her. [143]

Sola—schooner, "commanded by a Swede and manned by Chilians"; arrived _____, departed May 5, 1849 with S. S. Hill a passenger. [80]

Herald—H.M. ship, 26 guns, Capt. Henry Kellett in command; arrived May 9, 1849, departed May 19, 1849; Berthold Seemann, naturalist, aboard; in search of *Erebus* and *Terror* under Franklin. [159]

   Herald returned in 1850.

Amphitrite—H.M.S. frigate, 1076 tons, Capt. Rodney Eden; arrived May 22, 1849 with Robert Elwes a passenger; departed July 17, 1849. [62]

Caroline—"of Hobart Town," 98 tons, Capt. Carter, master; arrived _____, departed July 9, 1849 with Robert Elwes a passenger. [62]

* *Poursuivante*—French naval frigate, Rear Admiral Legoarant de Tromelin; arrived August 12, 1849, departed September 5, 1849 with Patrick Dillon, French consul, a passenger for San Francisco. Tromelin conducted a series of "reprisals" after presenting ten demands drawn up by Dillon. [1, 98a]

* *Gassendi*—French steam corvette, Faucon, commander; arrived

August 13, 1849, joining the *Poursuivante* at Honolulu, departed September 5, 1849. [1, 71, 98, 98a]

* *Honolulu*—American registry, schooner, Capt. Newell, master; arrived _____, departed September 11, 1849 with G. P. Judd, commissioner to foreign powers, and the two princes as passengers. [1, 71, 98, 98a]

George and Susan—American registry, whaler, Capt. White, master; arrived during 1849, departed _____; J. C. Mullet's first visit. [132]

Mullet tells of two other visits but omits the dates.

1850

Samuel Roberts—American schooner, Capt. Charles A. Falkenberg; arrived January 23, 1850, departed February 20, 1850. Albert Lyman aboard. [114a]

Hampton—American registry, merchant ship, 443 tons, Capt. Davis, master; arrived May 20, 1850, left June 12, 1850. [49]

Enterprise—H.M.S., about 500 tons, Capt. Richard Collinson in command; arrived June 24, 1850, departed June 30, 1850, in search of *Erebus* and *Terror; Investigator*, M'Clure, under Collinson. [39]

Enterprise came again in December 1850.

Bayonnaise—French naval corvette, Capt. Jurien de La Gravière; arrived June 29, 1850, departed July 4, 1850. [100]

Investigator—H.M.S., about 400 tons, Commander Robert M'Clure; arrived July 1, 1850, departed July 4, 1850; under Collinson on *Enterprise;* while in search of *Erebus* and *Terror* under Franklin, made the Northwest Passage. [8, 139]

Samuel Russell—American registry, ship, 92 tons, Charles P. Low, master; arrived July 1, 1850, departed July 16, 1850; in China trade. [71, 113]

Sea Breeze—American bark, Capt. George Newell, master; arrived August 14, 1850, departed September 26, 1850. [135a]

* *Noble*—American registry, brig, 207 tons, Capt. Robertson, master; arrived September 9, 1850 with G. P. Judd, commissioner to foreign powers, and the two princes as passengers; departed _____. [1, 98, 98a, 145]

Herald—H.B.M. ship, 26 guns, Capt. Henry Kellett in command;

arrived October 16, 1850, departed October 30, 1850; Berthold Seemann, naturalist, aboard; in search of *Erebus* and *Terror* under Franklin. [159]

Herald had visited Hawaii in 1849.

Jane Remorino—English registry, bark, "Spanish captain"; arrived December 10, 1850 with Fredrich Gerstaecker a passenger, departed December 11, 1850. [73]

* *Serieuse*—French naval corvette, Cosnier, commander; arrived December 13, 1850; stayed three months with M. Emile Perrin, French commissioner, who presented again the identical demands made by France in 1849 through Tromelin and Dillon. [1]

Enterprise—H.M.S., about 500 tons, Capt. Richard Collinson in command; arrived December 17, 1850, departed January 1, 1851 in search of *Erebus* and *Terror*. [39]

Enterprise had visited Hawaii in June 1850.

Emeline—New London, Conn., registry, Capt. Howard, master; arrived _____ 1850 with Stephen C. Masset a passenger, departed _____. [118]   The date is an arbitrary one fixed after careful reading of the text.

Odd Fellow—_____ registry, schooner, _____, master; arrived _____, departed _____ 1850 with Stephen C. Masset a passenger. [118]   The date is an arbitrary one fixed after careful reading of the text.

Mazeppa—_____ registry, "clipper-built ship of 170 tons," _____, master; arrived _____ 1850, departed _____ 1850; William Shaw on board. [161]   The year 1850 is the arbitrary date chosen for the *Mazeppa's* visit after careful reading of the text.

1851

Mary Dare—British brig, 149 tons, belonged to Hudson Bay Co., Mount, master; arrived January 6, 1851 with Henry Coke a passenger, departed _____. [38, 145]

Corsair—British registry, brig, Capt. Neal, master; arrived January 24 and departed January 28, 1851 with Henry Coke a passenger. [38]

————–———— registry, ———, master; arrived June 1851, departed July 1851 with John Guy Vassar, traveling for his health. [181]

Arco Iris—American registry, bark, 500 tons, Capt. George Coffin, master; arrived October 2, 1851, left November 23, 1851. [37]

Arctic—American registry, clipper ship, whaler, Capt. Chas. W. Gelett, master; visited the Hawaiian Islands several times during the whaling seasons of 1851 and 1852. [72]

1852

Emily Bourne—————, brig, John Mount Thain, owner and master; arrived February 20, 1852, departed March 24, 1852. [111a]

Citizen—New Bedford registry, whaleship, Thomas Howes Norton, master; arrived Hilo, April 20, 1852, departed May 5, 1852; subsequently wrecked in the Arctic. [82]

Eugenie—Swedish naval frigate, Capt. C. A. Virgin in command; first Swedish man-of-war to visit Hawaii; first visit—arrived June 22, 1852, departed July 3, 1852; second visit—arrived August 25, 1852, departed August 27, 1852; N. J. Andersson, naturalist, C. Skogman, Lieut. First Class and astronomer. [3, 71, 163, 163a]

1853

Sovereign of the Seas—American registry, clipper ship, Capt. McKay, master; arrived January 15, 1853, with G. W. Bates a passenger, departed February 8, 1853 for New York. [14, 71]

Emily—American registry, whaler, ———, master; arrived October 12, 1853, departed November 1, 1853, "Roving Printer," aboard. [155]

S. B. Wheeler—American registry, steamer (sidewheeler), 114 tons, Capt. Gus Ellis, master; arrived November 14, 1853 with T. Robinson Warren a passenger. [71, 185] Renamed *Akamai;* this was the first vessel owned by the Hawaiian Steam Navigation Co.

1854

N. B. Palmer—American registry, clipper ship, Charles P. Low, master; arrived February 24, 1854, departed April 23, 1854; in China trade. [71, 113]

Mississippi—U.S. steam frigate; Commander S. S. Lee in command; arrived October 23, 1854, departed November 8, 1854; John M. Kell, master. [71, 93]

1855

Restless—American, schooner, passenger vessel, Capt. Brown, master; arrived February 19, 1855 from San Francisco. Charles Victor Crosnier de Varigny aboard. [180a]

Fanny Major—American passenger vessel, Capt. Hays, master; arrived from San Francisco March 29, 1855; C. A. Egerstrom aboard. [58a]

South Boston—American whaleship from Fairhaven, Mass., 339 tons, Edward F. Randolph, master; arrived Hilo, Hawaii, April 19, 1855, departed April 28 on a whaling cruise to the South Seas with C.A. Egerstrom as passenger, returned to Honolulu July (1?), 1855. [58a, 71]

Yankee—American bark, passenger vessel, Capt Smith, master; arrived June 19, 1855, departed July (2?), 1855 with C. A. Egerstrom aboard. [58a, 71]

1857

Morning Star—American missionary packet, about 150 tons, Capt. Samuel G. Moore, master; carried supplies to missions in Micronesia; arrived at Honolulu on first visit April 24, 1857. This and three subsequent vessels financed by Sunday School children in United States and Hawaii. [21, 71, 184]

Yankee—American, bark, passenger vessel, Capt. Smith, master; arrived from San Francisco May 6, 1857; Theo H. Davies, passenger. [48a, 71]

Pearl—H.B.M. screw steamship, 21-gun corvette, Capt. Sotheby in command; arrived May 10, 1857, departed May 14, 1857; on duty in Pacific; Rev. Edward A. Williams, chaplain. [190]

Plumper—H.M.S. steam-sloop, Capt. George Henry Richards in command; arrived October 16, 1857, departed October 23, 1857 to survey Vancouver Island and adjacent coast; Lieut. Richard Charles Mayne an officer. [120]

1858

Merrimac—U.S.N. steam frigate, Commodore John C. Long in command; Henry Gilman, secretary to Long; arrived October 12, 1858, departed October 23, 1858. [71, 74a]

1859

Achilles—British registry, ship, Capt. Hart, master; arrived September 27, 1859 with passengers, including R. H. Dana, Jr., of *Mastiff*, which burned at sea; departed October 2, 1859 for Sydney. [48, 71]

Architect—American registry, whale bark, Capt. Fish, master; arrived October 23, 1859 from Arctic; departed November 16, 1859 with Richard Henry Dana, Jr., a passenger for San Francisco. [48, 71]

Milwaukee—American, passenger vessel, Capt. Rhoades; arrived November 1, 1859 from Melbourne, Australia, departed November 11, 1859. [190a]

March 5, 1860

Powhatan—U.S. Navy steam frigate, flagship of the East India Squadron, Capt. George F. Pearson in command; brought from Japan members of the first Japanese embassy to the United States. Arrived March 5, 1860, departed March 18, 1860. [90a, 132a, 192a]

Index of Vessels and Persons

Achilles; British registry, ship, Capt. Hart, master, 1859. [71]
   See also Dana.

* *Acteon;* British sloop of war, Lord Edward Russell, 1836. [1, 98a]

Active; _____ registry, "small schooner," Richard Charlton, master, 1823, 1825. [1, 60, 129]   *See also* Ellis, Rev. William.

Adams; see *John Adams.*

ADAMS, CAPT. _____; American, master of *Atahualpa*, 1805. See *Atahualpa.*

ADAMS, CAPT. ALEXANDER; _____, master of *Sylph*, 1819. [53a]

AGATE, ALFRED T.; American, draftsman and artist with Wilkes Exploring Expedition, 1840–1841. [189]

* *Aigle;* English registry, whaler, Capt. Valentine Starbuck, master, 1823. Departure of Kamehameha II for England. [1, 129]

Akamai; Hawaiian registry, steamer, formerly the *S. B. Wheeler;* first vessel owned by the Hawaiian Steam Navigation Co., 1853. See *S. B. Wheeler.*

* *Albatross;* American registry, ship. Under various masters, she was an important figure in early trade, approximately 1810–1816. See *Papers of Hawaiian Historical Society No. 8* for a brief review of her career.

* *Albert;* schooner of about 71 tons; better known as *Hooikaika* belonging to Kamehameha III; seized and renamed by Lord Paulet; sent in March 1843 to convey Alexander Simpson as bearer of dispatches to British Foreign Office. J. F. B. Marshall, a passenger, secret envoy of the king, carried counter dispatches. *See* "Hawaiian Maritime History" in

45

Thrum's *Hawaiian Annual* for 1890 for brief account of *Hooikaika's* history. [98a]

ALLEN, MISS A. J.; ———, compiler of book about Dr. Elijah White; did not visit Hawaii. [2]

* ALLEN, JOSEPH; American, master of *Maro*, 1820. See *Maro*.

ALLYN, CAPT. ———; ———, master of *Phoenix*, 1836. [140]

Alzire; French registry, brig, Capt. Darluc, 1828. [99]

America; American registry, ship, ———, master, 1822. [119]

American; see *Fair American*.

Amphitrite; H.M.S. frigate, 1076 tons, Capt. Rodney Eden, 1849. [62]

ANDERSON, PROF. JOHN HENRY; American, conjurer, arrived *Milwaukee*, 1859. [190a]

ANDERSSON, N. J.; Swedish, author and botanist; *Eugenie*, 1852. [3]

Ann; American registry, ———, master, 1802. [134]

ARAGO, JACQUES; French, author and draftsman with Freycinet's expedition, *Uranie*, 1819. [4, 5, 6, 7]

ARCHER, HENRY; ———, master of *Glide*, 1830. [137]

Architect; American registry, bark, Capt. Fish, master, 1859. [71] *See also* Dana.

Arco Iris; ——— registry, bark, 300 tons, Capt. George Coffin, master, 1851. [37]

Arctic; American registry, clipper ship, whaler, Capt. Chas. W. Gelett, master; visited the Hawaiian Islands several times during the whaling seasons of 1851 and 1852. [72]

Argentina; "mounted forty-four guns"; belonged to Independents of South America; commanded by Capt. Hippolyte Bouchard, 1818. [46, 124]   See also *Santa Rosa*.

* *Argonaut;* British registry, merchant vessel, James Colnett, master, 1791. *See* Colnett.

ARMSTRONG, ALEX.; British, author, naval surgeon on *Investigator*, 1850. [8]

ARMSTRONG, JAMES; American, captain in U.S. Navy, in command of *United States*, 1843; in command of *Savannah*, 1844. [2a, 71, 192]

Arrow; "owned by London merchants," Capt. Campbell, master, 1822. [182]

Artémise; French naval frigate, Post Capt. Laplace in command, 1839. [105]

* *Arthur;* "from Bengal," snow, trader, Henry Barber, master, 1796; was wrecked off point on Oahu which bears Barber's name. [1]

Astor, John Jacob; American merchant who unsuccessfully attempted to establish a fur-trading post on the Columbia River 1811–1813; never came to Hawaii, although his boats did: *Tonquin,* 1811; *Beaver,* 1812; *Lark,* 1813. [47, 69, 69a, 88, 154]

Astrolabe; French naval frigate, La Pérouse in command, 1786. [102, 103, 104]

Atahualpa; Boston registry, trader, 210 tons, Capt. Dixey Wildes, master in 1802 [11, 65], Capt. Adams, master in 1805 [160], Capt. John Suter, master in 1812, 1813 [84b]. Bought by the Russians in late 1813 and name changed to *Bering.* Wrecked off Kauai in the attempted Russian occupation of that island under Dr. Georg Anton Scheffer. For a discussion of her career, *see* "The Trading Voyages of the Atahualpa" by F. W. Howay in *The Washington Historical Quarterly* for January 1928.

Averick; American registry, whaleship, Capt. Edward Swain, master; brought fifth company of American missionaries, 1832. [31, 63, 115a]

* Bachelot, Alexis; ——, Catholic missionary; arrived on *Comet,* 1827, departed on *Waverly,* 1831; arrived on *Clementine,* 1837, departed on *Our Lady of Peace,* 1837. [1, 98, 98a, 158]

Bailey, Samuel G.; American, master of *Millwood,* 1815–1816. [12]

* *Balena;* New Bedford registry, Capt. Edmund Gardner; with *Equator,* first whaleship to visit Hawaiian Islands; in fall of 1819, while at anchor in Kealakekua Bay, caught a whale which yielded 110 barrels of oil. See *The Sailor's Magazine and Naval Journal,* August 1834.

Baltic; Nantucket registry, whaleship, Capt. Chadwick, master, 1831. [54]

* Barber, Henry; ——, master of *Arthur,* which was wrecked

in 1796 off a point on Oahu which was named "Barber's Point." [1]   For additional information, see "Captain Henry Barber of Barber's Point" by F. W. Howay in Forty-seventh Annual Report of The Hawaiian Historical Society for the Year 1938.

Barge; see Cleopatra's Barge.

BARKER, CAPT. S.; ———, master of Hamilton, 1836. [2]

* BARKLEY, CHARLES WILLIAM; English, master of Imperial Eagle, 1787; master of Halcyon, 1792. [84, 84a]

* BARKLEY, MRS. FRANCES HORNBY TREVOR; English, wife of Capt. Charles William Barkley; accompanied her husband to Hawaii on the Imperial Eagle, 1787, and the Halcyon, 1792. She left the earliest-known account of Hawaii written by a woman, and may have been the first Caucasian woman to visit the Islands. [84]

BARNARD, CAPT. ———; ———, master of Hobomok, 1835. [135]

BARNARD, CHARLES H.; American, author, marooned at Masafuero and rescued by the Millwood, Bailey, master; returned home by way of Hawaii, 1815–1816. [12]

* BARNETT, CAPT. ———; ———, master of Mercury, 1795. [84]

BARNETT, CAPT. THOMAS; English, master of Gustavus III, 1791. [13a]

BARRELL, GEORGE; American, seaman, author, arrived on Tamaahmaah, 1824; returned to New England on Owhyhee, 1827. [12a]

BARROT, ADOLPHE; French, author, with Capt. Vaillant on the Bonite, 1836. [13]   See also Vaillant.

BARTLETT, JOHN; American, author, seaman aboard Gustavus III, 1791. [13a]

BARTON, CAPT. ———; ———, master of The Boy, 1837. [135]

BATES, GEORGE WASHINGTON; American, author and traveler; arrived on Sovereign of the Seas, 1853, left on ———. [14, 71]

Bayonnaise; French naval corvette, Capt. Jurien de La Gravière, 1850. [100]

BEALE, THOMAS; British, author and surgeon, Kent, 1831; Sarah and Elizabeth, 1832. [15]

Beaver; American registry, 480 tons, Capt. Cornelius Sowles, master, 1812. Astor's second vessel. [47]   See also Astor.

BECHERVAISE, JOHN; *see* Quarter Master, Old, pseudonym. [148]

* *Becket;* Hawaiian registry, ———, ———, master, 1829–1830. *See* Boki

BEECHEY, FREDERICK WILLIAM; British, author, captain in British navy in command of *Blossom,* 1826, 1827. [16]

BELCHER, SIR EDWARD; British, author, British navy; supernumerary and assistant surveyor with Beechey on the *Blossom,* 1826, 1827 [16], captain in command of *Sulphur* and *Starling,* Kellett, 1837, 1839. [17, 80b] During his visit of 1837, Belcher became involved with Du Petit-Thouars concerning the return of the Catholic priests on the *Clementine.*

BELCHER, J. HENSHAW; American, author and officer of U.S. Navy, *Columbia,* 1839. [18] See also *Columbia,* U.S.N. frigate.

Belgrano; Peruvian brig of war, ———, master, 1823. [124]

* BELL, CAPT. C.; British, captain in British navy in command of *Hazard,* 1843, 1844. [71]

BELL, EDWARD; British, author, clerk on *Chatham,* 1792, 1793, 1794. [18a] See also *Chatham* and Vancouver, George.

BENNETT, GEORGE; British, coauthor with Daniel Tyerman; missionary, *Mermaid,* 1822. [177] *See also* Ellis, Rev. William.

BENNETT, FREDERICK DEBELL; British, author and zoologist, *Tuscan,* April 1834, October 1834, October 1835. [19]

BENNETT, CAPT. JAMES; American, master of *Bering* (formerly *Atahualpa*), 1814–1815. [84a, 84b, 144a]

BERESFORD, WILLIAM; British, supercargo on *Queen Charlotte,* Dixon, 1786, 1786–1787, 1787. The preface of Dixon's book acknowledges that the account was written by Beresford. [53]

Bering; formerly *Atahualpa,* purchased by the Russians late 1813; arrived October 1814, Capt. James Bennett, master; went aground off Waimea, Kauai, January 31, 1815. [84a, 84b, 144a]

Betsy; British registry, a privateer, ———, master, 1800. [134]

Bhering; Boston registry, bark, Capt. B. F. Snow, 1843. [109]

BILLE, STEEN ANDERSON; Danish, captain in Danish navy, in command of *Galathea,* 1846. Negotiated a Danish treaty with the Hawaiian government on October 16, 1846. [19a, 71, 152, 153]

BINGHAM, HIRAM; American, ordained missionary, arrived with

pioneer company on *Thaddeus,* 1820. See *Thaddeus.* Left Hawaii on *Flora,* 1840. [138] His book [20] has been consulted for data not found in "historical narratives."

BINGHAM, HIRAM, JR.; American, ordained missionary, stationed in the Gilbert Islands, wrote *Story of the Morning Star.* [21] See also *Morning Star.*

* BISHOP, CHARLES; ———, master of *Ruby,* 1795. [84]

* BISHOP, CHARLES REED; American, arrived on *Henry,* October 12, 1846; William L. Lee, a fellow passenger. [1, 71] Bishop was the founder of the Bank of Bishop, Bishop Museum, and C. R. Bishop Trust; Hawaii's first philanthropist.

BLACK, WILLIAM; Captain in British navy, master of *Raccoon,* 1814. [86a]

Blanchard; see *Harriet Blanchard.*

BLANCHARD, ANDREW; American, master of *Bordeaux Packet,* 1817 [85], and of *Thaddeus,* 1820. [81a, 112, 129, 155a, 172]

BLINN, CAPT. ———; ———, master of *Clementine,* 1837. [89b, 158]

BLINN, RICHARD D.; American, master of *Parthian,* 1828. [78, 91, 92]

Blonde; British Royal Navy frigate, Capt. George Anson Byron (or Lord Byron) in command, 1825; brought back the bodies of Kamehameha II and Kamamalu who had died of measles in London. Robert Dampier, artist and draftsman, Andrew Bloxam, naturalist, and James Macrae, botanist, were aboard. [22, 47a, 76, 116]

BLONDELLA, ———; ensign in French navy, artist with La Pérouse, 1786. [104]

Blossom; H.B.M. sloop, Capt. Frederick William Beechey in command, 1826, 1827; on a voyage of exploration in the north Pacific. [16, 148]

BLOXAM, ANDREW; British, author and naturalist with Lord Byron on *Blonde,* 1825. [22]

BOELEN, JACOBUS; Dutch, author, on the *Wilhelmina en Maria,* 1828. [23] Boelen's book is in Dutch and no translation has been found.

BOIT, JOHN; American, author, fifth mate on *Columbia,* Gray, 1792 [24], master of *Union,* 1795. [25]

* BOKI; Hawaiian high chief, member of Kamehameha II's suite

on voyage to England, 1823–1825. In an attempt to retrieve his debts by making a fortune in sandalwood, he made an expedition to the south, 1829, which ended disastrously. He and his vessel *Kamehameha* were mysteriously lost. The other boat, *Becket,* with a tale of catastrophe, returned in 1830. [1, 98, 98a]

BOLDUC, J.-B. Z.; French-Canadian, author, Catholic missionary to Columbia River; arrived on _____ 1842, departed on *Cawlitz,* 1842. [26]

Bonite; French naval corvette, 800 tons, Capt. Auguste Nicolas Vaillant in command on a government expedition, 1836. Two artists aboard: Barthelme Lauvergne and Théodore Auguste Fisquet. [13, 106, 181a]

Bordeaux; see *Ville de Bordeaux.*

Bordeaux Packet; American registry, brig, Andrew Blanchard, master, 1817; sold to Kalaimoku in December 1817. [85] *See also* Hunnewell.

Bordelais; French registry, "a three-masted vessel of 200 tons," M. Camille de Roquefeuil, master, 1819. [151]

* *Boston;* U.S. ship of war, Commander J. C. Long in command, 1843. [1, 71]

BOUCHARD, HIPPOLYTE; French, captain in command of *Argentina,* 1818; see *Santa Rosa.*

Boussole; French naval frigate, de Langle in command, with La Pérouse's expedition, 1786; *see* La Pérouse.

Boy; see *The Boy.*

BRACKENRIDGE, WM. D.; American, horticulturist and artist with Wilkes Exploring Expedition, 1840–1841. [189]

BREWER, CHARLES; American, author, a founder of C. Brewer & Co.; in his *Reminiscences* mentions the many voyages he made to Hawaii; he came first on the *Paragon,* 1823; became a business associate of James Hunnewell and Henry Augustus Peirce. [27, 85, 86]

* *Britannia;* first vessel built in Hawaii, constructed under Vancouver's supervision in February 1794. [125, 178, 179]

BROUGHTON, WILLIAM ROBERT; British, author, in British navy, lieut. in command under Vancouver of *Chatham,* 1792, *see* Vancouver; captain in command of *Providence,* 1798. [28]

BROWN, CAPT. _____; _____, master of *Osprey,* 1818. [85]

BROWN, CAPT. ———; ———, master of *Restless,* 1855. [180a]

BROWN, MR. ———; ———, master of *Port au Prince,* 1806. [117]

* BROWN, WILLIAM; English, trader, master of *Butterworth,* 1793; master of *Jackal,* 1794. He and Capt. Gordon of the *Prince Lee Boo* became involved in native intrigue and were killed by some Hawaiians in 1795. [1]   For a discussion of Brown, see "A Northwest Trader at the Hawaiian Islands" by Ralph S. Kuykendall in *The Quarterly of the Oregon Historical Society,* vol. 24, p. 111–131.

BRUCE, CAPT. ———; English, captain in British navy in command of *Imogene,* 1837; tried to help in trouble about Catholic priests; placed a copper tablet on stump of coconut tree at Kealakekua in memory of Capt. Cook. [79]

BUCK, PETER SMITH; American, master of *Planet,* 1849. [143]

* BUCKLE, CAPT. ———; master of *Daniel,* 1825. [1, 129]   See also *Daniel.*

BUNKER, ALEX. D.; American, master of *Ontario,* 1825, March 1826, September 1826. [29]

BURLING, ———; American, clerk of *Eliza,* 1799, and probable author of the ship's journal commonly referred to as "William Sturgis' Journal." [84c]

* *Butterworth;* English registry, trader, William Brown, master, 1793; *see* Brown, William.

BUYERS, JOHN; British, trader, master of *Margaret,* 1802–1803; part-owner of the vessel with John Turnbull. [176]

BYRON, GEORGE ANSON; English lord, captain in British Royal Navy in command of *Blonde,* 1825. [47a, 76].   See also *Blonde.*

California; Mexican registry, schooner, 18 tons, Falkland (Faughlan) master, 1837. [90, 158]

CAMPBELL, ARCHIBALD; Scotsman, author, seaman, befriended by Kamehameha I; arrived on *Neva,* 1809; departed on *Duke of Portland,* 1810. [30]

CAMPBELL, CAPT. ———; ———, master of *Arrow,* 1822. [182]

Canton; American registry, whaler, Capt. Abraham Gardner, master, 1829, 1830. [164]

Canton; American registry, whaleship, Capt. Dyke, master, 1845. [71, 165]

Caroline; British registry, cutter, 50 tons, formerly *Dragon;* purchased by Richard J. Cleveland, an American who changed the name to *Caroline*, 1799. [36, 84d]   Not to be confused with an earlier cutter *Caroline* also owned by Cleveland.

Caroline; "of Hobart Town," 98 tons, Capt. Carter, master, 1849. [62]

CARR, OVERTON; American, lieut. U.S.N., Wilkes Exploring Expedition, in command of *Oregon*, 1841; *see* Wilkes.

CARTER, CAPT. ———; ———, master of *Caroline*, 1849. [62]

* *Carysfort;* H.B.M. frigate, Capt. Lord George Paulet, 1843; *see* Paulet.

CASTLE, SAMUEL NORTHRUP; American, missionary, arrived with eighth company of American missionaries on *Mary Frazier*, 1837. En route, he drew a sketch and wrote a description of the ship's accommodations. [188a]

Cawlitz; British registry, bark, belonged to Hudson Bay Co., 1842. [26]   See also *Cowlitz*.

CHADWICK, CAPT. ———; ———, master of *Baltic*, 1831. [54]

CHAMBERLAIN, LEVI; American, author, business agent for the American mission, arrived with second company on *Thames*, 1823. [168]

CHAMISSO, ADELBERT VON; French-German, author, naturalist with Kotzebue's expedition, *Rurick*, 1816, 1817. [30a]

CHAPIN, MARY ANN TENNEY; American, author, wife of Dr. Alonzo Chapin, medical missionary; arrived with fifth company on *Averick*, 1832. [31]

Charlotte; see *Queen Charlotte*.

CHARLTON, RICHARD; British, master of the *Active*, 1823. [60] Arrived in 1825 on the *Active* as British Consul at Honolulu. A storm center during his term of office, his schemes continued to function after his departure on the *Maryland* in 1842 and were a primary cause of the temporary cession to Great Britain in 1843; *see* Paulet. [1, 71, 98, 98a]

Chatham; H.B.M. armed tender, 135 tons, Vancouver's expedition, Lieut. William Broughton in command, 1792; Lieut. Peter Puget in command, 1793, 1794. Thomas Heddington, midshipman and artist, and Edward Bell, clerk, 1792, 1793, 1794. Thomas Manby, master's mate, 1793, 1794. [18a, 116a]   *See also* Vancouver.

CHEEVER, REV. HENRY T.; American, author and traveler, *Wales*, 1843. [32]

Chelsea; American registry, clipper ship, whaler, Capt. B———, master, 1836. [50]

Chenamus; American registry, brig, Capt. Couch, master, 1844; Capt. Sylvester, master, 1845. [71, 81]

Cherub; British ship of war, Capt. Tucker, 1814. [146]   *See also* Gamble.

Chinchilla; ——— registry, brig, Capt. Meek, master, 1832. [137]

CHORIS, LOUIS; Russian of German descent, author and draftsman with Kotzebue, *Rurick*, 1816. [33]   *See also* Kotzebue.

Citizen; New Bedford registry, whaleship, Thomas Howes Norton, master, 1852; subsequently wrecked in the Arctic. [82]

CLARK, JOSEPH G.; American, author, seaman, U.S.N., Wilkes Exploring Expedition; *Vincennes*, 1840–1841, 1841. [34]

* CLARKE, CAPT. ELISHA; ———, master of *John Palmer*, 1827. [1]

CLASBY, CAPT. ———; ———, master of *Thames*, 1823. [168]

* *Clementine;* British registry, brig, owned by Jules Dudoit of Honolulu, Capt. Blinn and Capt. Handley, masters in 1837; Capt. Walker, master, 1840. [1, 89b, 98, 98a, 145, 158]

* *Cleopatra's Barge;* yacht of 191½ tons purchased by Kamehameha II in November 1820 for $90,000, to be paid for in sandalwood; renamed *Haaheo o Hawaii,* meaning *Pride of Hawaii;* for history see *Papers of the Hawaiian Historical Society No. 13.*

CLERKE, CHARLES; British, captain in British navy, with Cook on his third expedition, in command of *Discovery*, 1778, 1779; after Cook's death assumed command of expedition; died of consumption in Arctic regions shortly after leaving Hawaii; *see* Cook, James.

CLEVELAND, H. W. S.; American, author, wrote life of his father, Richard J. Cleveland, who came to Hawaii in 1799 and again in 1803. [35]

CLEVELAND, RICHARD J.; American, author, trader, master of *Caroline* or *Dragon*, 1799; partner of William Shaler, and supercargo of *Lelia Byrd*, 1803; brought first horse to Hawaii. [35, 36, 84d]   *See also* Shaler.

Columbia; Boston registry, ship, 250 tons, Robert Gray, master, 1789, 1792; a trader and the first American vessel to circumnavigate the globe, 1788–1789. [24]

Columbia; English registry, schooner, 185 tons, trader, Anthony Robson, master, January 1815; Capt. Jennings, master, December 1815, January 1817, December 1817; Peter Corney, chief officer on all visits; sold on May 2, 1818 to Kamehameha I. [46]

Columbia; British registry, Hudson Bay Co.'s bark, Capt. Darby, master, 1836. Rev. Samuel Parker arrived on her. [140, 158]

Columbia; British registry, Hudson Bay Co.'s bark, 300 tons, Capt. Royal, master, 1836. John K. Townsend arrived on her. [158, 175]

Columbia; English registry, bark, Capt. Humphries, master, 1844. Rev. Gustavus Hines arrived from Oregon on her. [81]

Columbia; U.S.N. frigate, Commodore George C. Read in command, 1839; accompanied by *John Adams,* Wyman. Read's visit helped to ease the tension caused by Laplace of the *Artémise.* [18, 133, 170]

COLVOCORESSES, GEORGE M.; American, author, lieut., U.S.N., Wilkes Exploring Expedition, *Vincennes,* 1840–1841, *Oregon,* 1841. [43]

* *Comet;* French registry, ship, Capt. Plassard, master, 1827; brought first Catholic missionaries. [1, 98, 98a]

* *Congaree;* American registry, ship, Capt. Weston, master, 1844. [89b, 145]

Congress; U.S. frigate, Commodore Robert F. Stockton, 1846. [41, 42, 71, 180]

* *Constellation;* U.S.N. frigate, Commodore L. Kearney, 1843. [71]

Constitution, "Old Ironsides"; U.S. frigate, Capt. John Percival, 1845. [71, 167]

COOK, JAMES; British, author, captain in British navy in command of his third voyage of discovery; *Resolution* and *Discovery,* Clerke; discovered Sandwich Islands January 18, 1778; on his second visit, killed at Kealakekua, Hawaii, February 14, 1779. [44, 44a, 59, 64a, 74, 108, 150, 157, 193, 193a]

from this ship attacked Mr. Richards' house at Lahaina. The incident is sometimes called "the first Lahaina outrage." [1, 129]

DARBY, CAPT. ——; ——, master of Hudson Bay Co.'s bark *Columbia*, 1836. [140, 158]

Dare; see *Mary Dare.*

DARLUC, CAPT. ——; French, master of *Alzire*, 1828. [99]

DAVIES, THEOPHILUS HARRIS; British, merchant, author, founder of Theo H. Davies & Co., Ltd.; arrived on *Yankee* from San Francisco, 1857. [48a]

DAVIS, CAPT. ——; American, master of *Hampton*, 1850. [49]

* DAVIS, ISAAC; English, survivor of massacre of *Fair American's* crew, 1790. Davis became one of Kamehameha I's chief advisors. *See* Metcalf, Simon.

DAVIS, JOHN SHEDDON; Scotsman, probable author of a log of the *Emily Bourne*, 1852. [111a]

DAVIS, R. C.; American, author, captain's son, *Hampton*, 1850. [49]

DAVIS, CAPT. WILLIAM HEATH; American, master of *Isabella*, 1813. [84a, 149a]

DAVIS, WILLIAM M.; American, author, seaman, *Chelsea*, 1836. [50]

DELANO, AMASA; American, author, master of *Perseverance*, 1801, 1806. [51]

DELANO, REUBEN; American, author, seaman, *Stanton*, 1825, 1826. [52]

Diamond; "from England," bark, Capt. Fowler, master, 1843. [109]

Diana; American registry, brig, Capt. Hinckley, master, 1837. [2, 158]

* DILLON, PATRICK; French consul at Honolulu; arrived on *Sarcelle*, 1848, departed on *Poursuivante*, 1849. During his short stay in these islands, Dillon was the center of disturbance between France and Hawaii. [1, 71, 98, 98a]

Discovery; H.B.M. sloop, 300 tons, Capt. James Cook's third voyage, commanded successively by Capt. Clerke, Capt. Gore, and Capt King, 1778, 1779. *See* Cook, James.

Discovery; H.B.M. sloop, 350 tons, Capt. George Vancouver,

1792, 1793, 1794; *see* Vancouver. Thomas Manby, master's mate on board, 1792. [116a]

Discovery (Otkrytie); see Scheffer.

DIXON, GEORGE; British, author, with Cook on his last voyage, 1778, 1778–1779; under Portlock in command of *Queen Charlotte* 1786, 1786–1787, 1787. [53] *See also* Portlock.

* DOANE, CAPT. ——; ——, master of *Sarah Abigail*, 1842. [129]

* DOANE, CAPT. ——; ——, master of *Globe*, 1844. [129]

DOBELL, PETER (PIERRE DOBEL); born in Ireland, served in American army, became Russian citizen; merchant, sometime consul, author; arrived on *Sylph*, 1819. [53a]

DODGE, GEORGE A.; American, author, seaman on *Baltic*, 1831. [54]

Dolphin; U.S. schooner, Lieut. John Percival in command, 1826. [107, 142]

Don Quixote; Hawaiian registry, bark, Capt. John Paty, master, 1840. [66, 67, 98a]

DORR, EBENEZER; American, master of *Otter*, 1796–1797. [144] *See also* Péron.

DOUGLAS, DAVID; Scotsman, author, eminent botanist, first visit—arrived in August 1832; second visit—arrived in December 1833; the following July, killed on the island of Hawaii. A tablet to his memory placed on the exterior of Kawaiahao church in Honolulu. [55, 56]

DOUGLAS, WILLIAM; ——, owner and master of *Grace*, 1790; formerly first mate of *Lady Washington*. [84a, 87]

DOUGLAS, WILLIAM; British, under John Mcares, master of *Iphigenia*, 1788–1789, 1789; *see* Meares.

DOWNES, JOHN; American, commodore in U.S. Navy in command of *Potomac*, 1832. [137, 149, 186]

Dragon; see *Caroline.*

DRAYTON, JOSEPH; American, draftsman and artist with Wilkes Exploring Expedition, 1840–1841. [189]

Dromo; American registry, trader, 600 tons, Capt. W——, master, 1809. [111]

* *Dublin;* H.B.M. flagship, Rear Admiral Richard Thomas, 1843; *see* Paulet.

DUHAUT-CILLY, AUGUSTE BERNARD; French, author, master of *Heros*, 1828. [57, 109a]

Duke of Portland; "South-Sea whaler, bound for England," Capt. Spence, master, 1810. [30]

DUNCAN, CAPT. ———; ———, master of *Vancouver*, 1839. [66, 67]

* DUNCAN, CHARLES; British, master of *Princess Royal*, 1788. *See* Colnett.

DU PETIT-THOUARS, ABEL; French, author, capt. in French navy in command of *Vénus*, 1837. [58] With Belcher on the *Sulphur*, Du Petit-Thouars became involved concerning the return of the Catholic priests on the *Clementine*. He signed a treaty assuring French subjects equal rights with other foreigners.

DYKE, CAPT. ———; ———, master of *Canton*, 1845. [71, 165]

EALES, CAPT. ———; ———, master of *Ganymede*, 1835. [109]

* EASTABROOK, CAPT. ———; ———, master of *Gloucester*, 1841, 1842. [89b, 129, 158]

EBBETS (EBETTS), CAPT. JOHN; American, first mate of *Alert*, 1800, master of *Alert*, 1802; master of *Pearl*, 1805, 1806; master of *Enterprise*, 1811, 1816–1818. Appears to have become a resident of Honolulu. [84a, 84e, 98a, 141]

EDEN, RODNEY; British, captain in British navy, in command of *Amphitrite*, 1849. [62]

EDGAR, THOMAS; British, author, lieut. with Cook's third expedition, 1778, 1779. [44a] *See also* Cook, James.

EGERSTROM, CHARLES AXEL; Swedish, adventurer, author, arrived on *Fanny Major*, sailed on whaling cruise to the South Seas on *South Boston*, departed from Honolulu on *Yankee*, 1855. [58a, 71]

* *Eleanora;* American registry, brig, 190 tons, Simon Metcalf, master, 1790. *See* Metcalf, Simon.

Eliza; Boston registry, 159 tons, Capt. James Rowan, master, 1799. [84c]

ELLIS, GUS; ———, master of *S. B. Wheeler*, 1853. [71, 185]

ELLIS, WILLIAM; British, author, artist, assistant surgeon with Cook's third expedition on *Discovery*, 1778, 1779. [44a, 59]

ELLIS, REV. WILLIAM; British, author, missionary in Tahiti; first visit—a fellow passenger of Tyerman and Bennet [177] on

Mermaid, 1822; second visit—arrived on *Active*, 1823, departed on *Russell*, 1824. [60, 61, 129] Because of the similarity of the Tahitian and Hawaiian languages, Ellis was of great assistance to the American missionaries.

ELWES, ROBERT; British, author, traveler and artist; arrived *Amphitrite*, 1849, departed, *Caroline*, 1849. [62]

* *Embuscade;* French corvette, Capt. Mallet, 1842; *see* Mallet.

Emeline; New London, Conn., registry, schooner, Capt. Howard, master, 1850. [118]

EMERSON, OLIVER POMEROY; American, author, son of John and Ursula Emerson, missionaries who came with fifth company on the *Averick*, 1832, and whose journals of that voyage form a part of their son's book. [63]

Emily; American registry, whaler, _____, master, 1853. [155]

Emily Bourne; _____, brig, Capt. John Mount Thain, owner-master, 1852. [111a]

* *England;* see *New England.*

Enterprise; U.S. naval schooner, Capt. George N. Hollins in command under Commodore Kennedy, 1836. [156, 158]

Enterprise; H.M.S., about 500 tons, Capt. Richard Collinson in command, June 1850, December 1850. [39]

Enterprise; see *Predpriatie.*

Enterprise; American, "of New York," 291 tons, general trader owned by John Jacob Astor, Capt. John Ebbets, master, 1811, 1816–1818. [84e]

* *Equator;* Nantucket registry, Capt. Elisha Folger, 1819; see *Balena.*

Erebus and *Terror;* British vessels under Sir John Franklin lost while exploring the Arctic regions; did not visit Hawaii but boats sent in search of them did; see *Plover, Herald, Enterprise* (H.M.S.), *Investigator.*

Ermak; see *Yarmouth.*

ERSKINE, CHARLES; American, author, seaman, U.S.N., Wilkes Exploring Expedition, *Vincennes*, 1840–1841, 1841. [64]

Eugenie; Swedish naval frigate, Capt. C. A. Virgin in command; 1852. [3, 71, 163, 163a] First Swedish man-of-war to visit Hawaiian Islands.

Euphemia; Hawaiian registry, brig, Capt. Thomas Russum, master, 1847. [115]

Europa; American registry, ship, Capt. Shaw, master, January–March 1837; John Townsend, an outbound passenger. [175] November 1837, Maigret and Murphy, Catholic missionaries inbound passengers. [158]

* *Fair American;* American registry, tender, Thomas Metcalf, master, 1790; *see* Metcalf, Simon.

FALKENBERG, CHARLES A.; American, master of schooner *Samuel Roberts,* 1850. [114a]

FALKLAND, ———; Irish, owner of *California,* 1837. [90]   Listed as its master (Faughlan) in *Sandwich Island Gazette.* [158]

* *Fama;* American registry, ship, Capt. Cornelius Hoyer, master, 1839. [89b, 98a, 158]

Fanny Major; American passenger vessel, bark, Capt. Hays, master, 1855. [58a, 71]

FARNHAM, THOMAS J.; American, lawyer, traveler, Hawaii's first commissioner aboard; arrived *Vancouver,* 1839, left on *Don Quixote,* 1840. [66, 67, 98a]

* FAUCON, ———; French, commander of *Gassendi,* 1849. [1, 71]

FAUGHLAN; *see* Falkland.

Fawn; British registry, ship, Capt. Dale, master, 1825. [168]

Felice; British registry, 230 tons, John Meares, master, 1788. [121, 122, 123]

FINCH, WILLIAM; American, captain in U.S. Navy, in command of *Vincennes,* 1829. [169]

FISH, CAPT. ———; ———, master of *Architect,* 1859. [71]   *See also* Dana.

FISQUET, THÉODORE AUGUSTE; French, artist with French government expedition, *Bonite,* 1836. [181a]

FLEURIEU, C. P. CLARET; French, author of account of Marchand's voyage on *Solide,* 1791; did not visit Hawaii. [68]

FLEURY, ———; ———, master of the *Mary,* 1849. [114]

Flora; American registry, bark, merchant vessel, Capt. Spring, master, 1840. [138]

Flying Fish; U.S.N. tender, 96 tons; Commandant Samuel Knox, Wilkes Exploring Expedition; 1840, 1841; *see* Wilkes.

* FOLGER, ELISHA; American, master of *Equator,* 1819; see *Balena.*

Foster; Nantucket registry, ship, ———, master, 1823. [124]

FOWLER, CAPT. ———; ———, master of *Diamond,* 1843. [109]

FRANCHÈRE, GABRIEL; French Canadian, author and clerk in Astor's enterprise, *Tonquin*, 1811. [69, 69a] *See also* Astor.

FRANKLIN, SAMUEL R.; American, author, U.S.N. midshipman on *United States*, 1843; afterwards an admiral. [70, 71]

FRANKLIN, SIR JOHN; see *Erebus* and *Terror*.

* *Frazier;* see *Mary Frazier.*

Freeling; see *Henry Freeling.*

FREYCINET, LOUIS DE; French, captain in command of a French exploring and scientific expedition, *Uranie*, 1819. [4, 5, 6, 7, 70a, 70b]

FREYCINET, MADAME ROSE DE SAULCES DE; French, author, wife of Louis de Freycinet, *Uranie*, 1819. [70a, 70b]

FROST, JOSEPH H.; American, coauthor with Daniel Lee; Methodist missionary to Oregon; *Lausanne*, 1840, Gustavus Hines a fellow passenger [81]; second visit, arrived *Diamond*, 1843, departed *Bhering*, 1843. [109]

FUNTER, ROBERT; British, master of *North West America*, 1788–1789; *see* Meares.

Galathea; Danish naval corvette, 26 guns, Capt. Steen Anderson Bille in command, 1846. [19a, 71, 152, 153]

GAMBLE, JOHN; American, lieut. in U.S. Marine Corps in command of *Sir Andrew Hammond*, a British letter of marque ship captured by the Americans, consequently the first war vessel flying U.S. flag to enter Honolulu harbor, 1814. Shortly after leaving, retaken by the British ship *Cherub*, Capt. Tucker. Lieut. Gamble left as a prisoner of war on the *Cherub*. [146] *See also* "John M. Gamble" by Edwin North McClellan in *Thirty-Fifth Annual Report of The Hawaiian Historical Society for the Year 1926.*

Ganymede; bark owned by Hudson Bay Co., Capt. Eales, master, 1835. [109]

* *Garafilia;* American registry, brig, Seymour, master, 1836. [158] *See* Walsh.

GARDNER, CAPT. ⸺ ; ⸺, master of *Rosellic*, March and fall of 1826, March and September of 1827. [135]

GARDNER, ABRAHAM; ⸺, master of *Canton*, 1829, 1830. [164]

* GARDNER, EDMUND; American, master of *Balena*, 1819; see *Balena.*

* *Gassendi;* French steam corvette, Faucon, 1849; at Honolulu joined *Poursuivante.* [1, 71, 98a]   *See also* Tromelin.

GELETT, CHARLES WETHERBY; American, author, in the whaling industry for many years; master of *India,* 1841; of *Uncas,* 1844–1845, 1847–1848; of *Arctic,* 1851–1852. [72]

George; see *King George.*

George and Susan; American registry, whaler, Capt. White, master, 1849. [132]

GERSTAECKER, FRIEDRICH WILHELM CHRISTIAN; German, author and traveler; arrived *Jane Remorino,* 1850, left on a German whaler, name and date not given. [73]

GILBERT, GEORGE; British, with Cook on his third voyage, on *Discovery,* 1778, 1779; "by successive deaths of Captain Cook and Captain Clerke he was promoted to be lieutenant." [74] *See also* Cook, James.

GILMAN, WILLIAM HENRY; American, author, secretary to Commodore John C. Long, *Merrimac,* 1858. [74a]

Glide; American registry, ———, Capt. Henry Archer, master, 1830. [137]

Globe; Nantucket registry, whaleship, Thomas Worth, master, 1823. The crew mutinied and the two survivors, Wm. Lay and Cyrus Hussey, were rescued by the *Dolphin.* [107, 142] *See also* Percival.

* *Globe;* "from Boston," brig, Capt. Doane, master; brought eleventh company of American missionaries, 1844. [71]

* *Gloucester;* "from Boston," ship, Capt. Eastabrook, master; brought ninth company of American missionaries, 1841. [129] James Jackson Jarves left aboard her, 1842. [89b, 158]

GOLOVNIN, VASILII MIKHAILOVICH; Russian, author, captain in Russian navy in command of *Kamchatka,* 1818. [74b, 75]

* GORDON, CAPT. ———; British, master of *Prince Lee Boo,* 1794. *See* Brown, William.

* GORDON, CAPT. ———; British, master of *Cormorant,* 1846. [71, 145]

GORE, JOHN; born in America, author, in British navy on Cook's third voyage; went out a lieutenant on *Resolution,* at Cook's death promoted to captain in command of *Discovery,* and at Clerke's death assumed command of *Resolution,* 1778, 1779. [44, 44a]

Grace; of New York, schooner, 85 tons, William Douglas, owner and master, 1790. [84a, 87]

GRAHAM, MRS. MARIA; ———, did not visit Hawaii, compiler of account of the voyage of the *Blonde*, 1825. [76]

GRAVIERE, JURIEN DE LA; *see* La Gravière, Jurien de.

GRAY, ROBERT; American, master of *Columbia*, 1789, 1792. [24] Gray was the first American to circumnavigate the globe, 1788–1789. He also discovered the mouth of the Columbia River.

GREEN, JONATHAN SMITH; American, author, missionary, arrived on *Parthian*, 1828. He left on *Volunteer*, February 1829 for Northwest Coast to report on a possible new field in which the American Board might open a new mission, and returned November 1829. [77]

GREEN, THEODOSIA ARNOLD; American, wife of Jonathan Smith Green, missionary, arrived on *Parthian*, 1828. [78]

GREENE, DANIEL; American, master of *Neptune*, 1798. [174]

GREGORY, HERBERT E.; American, coauthor with Ralph S. Kuykendall. Their book [98] has been consulted for data not found in "historical narratives."

Gustavus III; formerly the British snow *Mercury* but "flying Swedish colors," 152 tons, Capt. Thomas Barnett, master, 1791. [13a, 84a]

Haaheo o Hawaii; see *Cleopatra's Barge.*

* HAALILIO, TIMOTHY; Hawaiian, departed with William Richards on mission to foreign powers on *Shaw*, 1842; died on *Montreal* during return voyage in 1844–1845. [1, 98, 98a, 145]

HAGEMEISTER, CAPT. LEONTII ANDREANOVICH; officer in Russian navy, in command of *Neva*, 1809. [30, 144a]

* *Halcyon;* British registry, brig, Charles William Barkley, master, 1792. [84, 84a]

* HAMELIN, REAR ADMIRAL; French, in command of *Virginie*, 1846; restored the $20,000 taken by Capt. Laplace in 1839. [1, 71, 98, 98a]

Hamilton; Boston registry, Capt. Porter, master, 1806. [141]

Hamilton; American registry, ship, Capt. S. Barker, master, 1836. [2]

Hammond; see *Sir Andrew Hammond.*

Hampton; American registry, merchant ship, 443 tons, Capt. Davis, master, 1850. [49]

* *Hancock;* American registry, brig, 157 tons, Capt. Samuel Crowell, master, 1791. [84, 84a]

Hancock; "of Boston," trader, Capt. Crocker, master, 1799. [84d]

Harriet Blanchard; ——— registry, schooner, Capt. Levi Young, master, 1830. [164]

HART, CAPT. ———; ———, master of *Achilles,* 1859. [71]   *See also* Dana.

HAY, SIR JOHN C. DALRYMPLE; English, author, British navy, midshipman on *Imogene,* 1837. [79]   Hay became an admiral. *See also* Bruce.

HAYS, CAPT. ———; American, master of *Fanny Major,* 1855. [58a, 71]

* *Hazard;* H.B.M. ship, Capt. Bell, 1843, 1844. [71]

HEDDINGTON, THOMAS; British, midshipman and artist with Vancouver, *Chatham,* 1792, 1793, 1794. [125, 178, 179]

HEDGES, CAPT. ———; ———, master of *Josephine,* 1849. [71, 80]

* *Hellespont;* "from Boston," ship, Capt. Henry, master; brought seventh company of American missionaries, 1835. [129]

* *Henry;* American registry, brig, Capt. Kilborn, master, 1846. [71]

* HENRY, CAPT. ———; ———, master of *Hellespont,* 1835. [129]

Henry Freeling; British registry, 101 tons, Capt. Keen, master, 1835–1836. [187]

Herald; H.M. ship, 26 guns, Capt. Henry Kellett in command, 1849, 1850, in search of *Erebus* and *Terror* under Franklin. [159]

HERGEST, ———; British, lieut. in command under Vancouver of *Daedalus,* 1792. On May 11, 1792, Hergest and two others were killed by natives at Waimea, Oahu. [179]

Heros; French registry, commercial vessel, 370 tons, Capt. Abel Duhaut-Cilly, master, 1828. [57, 109a]

HILL, CAPT. SAMUEL; American, author, master and supercargo of *Ophelia,* 1816. [80a]

HILL, SAMUEL S.; English, author, traveler; arrived on *Josephine,* 1848, left on *Sola,* 1849. [71, 80]

HINCKLEY, CAPT. ———; ———, master of *Diana,* 1837. [2]

HINDS, RICHARD BRINSLEY; British, author and artist, surgeon on the *Sulphur,* 1837, 1839. [80b]

HINES, REV. GUSTAVUS; American, author, Methodist missionary to Oregon; first visit—*Lausanne,* 1840, Joseph H. Frost, a fellow passenger [109]; second visit—arrived from Oregon on *Columbia,* 1844, John Ricord a fellow passenger [71], left on *Chenamus,* 1844; third visit—arrived on *Chenamus,* 1845, left on *Leland,* 1845. [81]

Hobomok; American registry, whaler, Capt. Barnard, master, 1835. [135]

HOLLINS, GEORGE N.; American, captain in U.S. Navy in command under Commodore Kennedy of *Enterprise,* 1836. [156, 158]

* HOLLIS, CAPT. ———; ———, master of *Samoset,* 1848. [71]

HOLMAN, LUCIA RUGGLES; American, author, wife of missionary physician Dr. Thomas Holman; arrived with pioneer company of American missionaries on *Thaddeus,* 1820. Dr. and Mrs. Holman left Hawaii October 2, 1821, on *Mentor,* Capt. Lemuel Porter, for the United States via Canton, China. ". . . it is believed that Mrs. Holman was one of the first American women, if not the earliest, to circumnavigate the globe." [81a, 84a]

HOLMES, REV. LEWIS; American, author, did not visit Hawaii but wrote account of voyage of *Citizen,* 1852. [82]

* *Honolulu;* American registry, schooner, Capt. Fisher Ames Newell, master, 1849. [1, 71, 98, 98a, 135a]

* *Hooikaika;* schooner of about 71 tons belonging to Kamehameha III; during Lord Paulet's supremacy her name changed to *Albert.* [98a] See *Albert.*

HOOPER, WILLIAM HULME; British, author, lieut. in British navy, *Plover,* 1848, in search of *Erebus* and *Terror* under Franklin. [83]

Hope; American registry, brigantine, 70 tons, trader, Joseph Ingraham, master, May 1791 and October 1791. [87]

HOWARD, CAPT. ———; ———, master of *Emeline,* 1850. [118]

HOWAY, FREDERIC WILLIAM; Canadian judge and historian, died 1943. His address delivered during the Cook Sesquicentennial Celebration in Hawaii in 1928 is included because it describes voyages to Hawaii before 1800 about which little is known. His "List of Trading Vessels . . ." is included as a valuable source for descriptions of vessels, names of captains, and dates. [84, 84a, 84b, 84c, 84d, 84e, 149a, 193a]

HOWLAND, CAPT.; ——, master of *Stanton*, 1825, 1826. [20, 52]

HOYER, CAPT. CORNELIUS; American, master of *Fama*, 1839. [89b, 158]

HUDSON, JOHN; American, master of *Tamana*, 1805, 1806. [141, 160]

HUDSON, WILLIAM L.; American, captain in U.S.N. Wilkes Exploring Expedition, in command of *Peacock*, 1840. *See* Wilkes.

HUMPHRIES, CAPT. ——; ——, master of *Columbia*, 1844. [81]

HUNNEWELL, JAMES; American, author; first visit—arrived on *Bordeaux Packet*, 1817, left as passenger on *Osprey*, 1818 [85]; second visit—first officer on *Thaddeus*, 1820; third visit —master of *Missionary Packet*, 1826 [86]; became business associate of Charles Brewer and Henry A. Peirce. [27]

Huntress; American registry, whaler, Capt. Post, master, 1833, 1834. [173]

HUSSEY, CYRUS; American, coauthor with William Lay; a cooper on *Globe*, 1823, *Dolphin*, 1826. [107] See also *Globe*.

Ilmen; see Scheffer.

Imogene; H.M.S. frigate, 26 guns, Capt. Bruce in command, 1837. [79]

* *Imperial Eagle* or *Loudoun;* "British ship flying Austrian colors," 400 tons, in fur trade, Charles William Barkley, master, 1787. [84]

Independence; U.S. ship, Com. Shubrick, 1848. [71, 191]

India; American registry, whaleship, Capt. Chas. W. Gelett, master, 1841. [72]

INGRAHAM, JOSEPH; American, author; second mate of *Columbia*, Gray, 1789; master of *Hope*, May 1791 and October 1791. [87]

Investigator; H.M.S., about 400 tons, Commander Robert M'Clure, 1850; while in search of *Erebus* and *Terror* under Sir John Franklin, made the Northwest Passage. [8, 139]

Iphigenia; British registry, ship, 200 tons, William Douglas, master; one of John Meares' vessels, 1788–1789, accompanied by *North West America*, 1789. *See* Meares.

Iris; see Arco Iris.

IRVING, WASHINGTON; American, author, wrote *Astoria* at request of Astor to tell story of Astor's unsuccessful enterprise; never visited Hawaii. [88] *See also* Astor.

Isabella; Boston-owned ship, 209 tons, trader, Capt. William Heath Davis, master in 1813; Capt. Tyler, master in 1815 when it brought Dr. Georg Anton Scheffer to Hawaii. [84a, 144a, 149a]

ISELIN, ISAAC; American, author, supercargo on *Maryland,* 1807. [89]

* *Jackal;* English registry, schooner, trader, Alexander Stewart, master, 1793; Capt. William Brown, master, 1794. [1, 98a] *See also* Kendrick.

Jane; —— registry, 100 tons, ——, master, 1795. [134]

Jane Remorino; English registry, bark, "Spanish captain," 1850. [73]

Japan; British registry, Capt. John May, master, employed in sperm whale fishery, 1832. Robert Jarman, seaman aboard. [89a]

JARMAN, ROBERT; English, author, seaman aboard whaleship *Japan,* 1832. [89a]

JARVES, JAMES JACKSON; American, author, first editor of the newspaper *Polynesian.* Made three trips to Hawaii: arrived on *Peru* and departed on *Clementine,* 1837; arrived on *Fama,* 1839, departed on *Gloucester,* 1842; arrived on *Congaree,* 1844, departed on *Starling,* 1848. [89b, 98a, 145, 158]

* *Jefferson;* American registry, ship, Capt. Roberts, master, 1793, 1794. [84]

JENKINS, JAMES; American, author, supercargo, *California,* 1837. [90, 158]

JENNINGS, CAPT. JOHN; English, master of *Columbia,* December 1815, January 1817, December 1817. [46]

* *Jenny;* "of Bristol, England," three-masted schooner, Capt. Baker, master, 1792; captured two natives who were returned by Vancouver the next year. [1, 84]

John Adams; U.S.N. sloop, Capt. Thomas Wyman in command, 1839; accompanied *Columbia* under Commodore Read. See *Columbia,* U.S. frigate.

* *John Palmer;* British registry, whaler, Capt. Elisha Clarke, master, 1827. Sailors from this vessel made an assault at Lahaina, sometimes called "the third Lahaina outrage." [1]

JOHNSON, CAPT. ———; ———, master of *Mastiff*, 1859. *See* Dana.

JOHNSTON, JAMES D.; American, author, lieut. in U.S. Navy, executive officer of *Powhatan* and charged with the care of the Japanese embassy, 1860. [90a, 132a, 192a]

JONES, THOMAS AP CATESBY; American, U.S.N., captain in command of *Peacock*, 1826; settled American claims and generally produced a better feeling between the United States and Hawaii; came again as commodore in command of *United States*, 1843. [1, 70, 71, 98, 98a]

Josephine; American registry, whaleship, Capt. Hedges, master, 1848. [71, 80]

JUDD, GERRIT PARMELE; American, author, medical missionary, arrived with third company on *Parthian*, 1828. [91] See also *Parthian*. Dr. Judd left the mission in 1842 to become the advisor of the king and chiefs. As commissioner to foreign powers, he left with the two princes on the *Honolulu*, 1849, and returned on the *Noble*, 1850. [1, 71, 98, 98a]

JUDD, LAURA FISH; American, author, wife of Dr. Gerrit Parmele Judd, arrived with third company of missionaries on *Parthian*, 1828. [92]

KAIANA (TIANNA); Hawaiian chief who went to China on *Nootka*, John Meares, master, 1787, and returned on *Iphigenia*, William Douglas, master, 1788. *See* Meares.

* *Kamehameha;* Hawaiian registry, brig, 1829. *See* Boki.

* *Kamehameha III;* "schooner yacht" built in 1845 in Baltimore and fitted for royal use; arrived March 8, 1846, Capt. Fisher Ames Newell, master. Purchased by King Kamehameha III and, when not in royal service, employed as weekly packet between Lahaina and Honolulu. [135a]

Kamchatka or *Kamschatka;* Russian sloop of war, Capt. Golovnin, 1818. [74b, 75]

* *Kanrin Maru;* Japanese warship, steam corvette, 192 tons, Admiral Katsu Rintaro in command, "escorted" the *Powhatan*, 1860. First Japanese vessel to cross the Pacific. *Kanrin Maru* did not stop in Honolulu, but sailed direct to San Francisco. [90a, 132a, 192a]

* KEARNEY, LAWRENCE; American, commodore in U.S. Navy in command of *Constellation*, 1843. [71, 127a]

KEEN, CAPT. ———; ———, master of *Henry Freeling*, 1835–1836. [187]

KELL, JOHN MCINTOSH; American, author, in U.S. Navy, midshipman on *Savannah*, 1845; master on *Mississippi*, 1854. [71, 93]

KELLETT, HENRY; British, in British navy, lieut. in command under Capt. Edward Belcher of *Starling*, 1837, 1839 [17]; captain in command of *Herald*, 1849, 1850. [159]

KELLINGTON, T. ———; ———, master of *Leland*, 1845. [71, 81]

* KENDRICK, JOHN; American, trader, master of *Lady Washington*, 1791, 1794. Considered the founder of the sandalwood trade between Hawaii and China. In 1794, he was killed while aboard the *Lady Washington* in Honolulu harbor by a wad of shot from the *Jackal* fired in celebration of a native victory. [1, 84a, 98, 98a]

KENNEDAY, SAMUEL; American, master of *Tsar*, 1848. [188]

KENNEDY, EDMUND P.; American, commodore in U.S. Navy in command of East India and Asiatic Squadron; *Peacock* and *Enterprise*, Hollins, 1836. [156, 158]

Kent; British registry, whaler, Capt. ———, 1831. [15]

KENT, CAPT. ———; British, master of *Mermaid*, 1822; convoyed *Prince Regent*, 1822. [60, 61, 177]

* KILBORN, CAPT. ———; ———, master of *Henry*, 1846. [71]

KILHAM, CAPT. G. E.; American, master of *Peru*, 1837. [89b, 158]

KING, JAMES; British, coauthor with Cook, in the British navy, on Cook's third voyage; went out a lieutenant on *Resolution*, returned a captain in command of *Discovery*, 1778, 1779. [44, 44a] *See also* Cook, James.

King George; British registry, 320 tons, Capt. Nathaniel Portlock in command, 1786, 1786–1787, 1787; *see* Portlock.

KNOX, SAMUEL; American, commandant U.S.N., Wilkes Exploring Expedition, in command of *Flying Fish*, 1840, 1841. *See* Wilkes.

Kodiak or *Myrtle*; *see* Scheffer.

KOTZEBUE, OTTO VON; Russian, author, in Russian navy, cadet with Krusenstern on *Nadeshda*, 1804 [97]; lieut. in command of *Rurick*, 1816, 1817 [30a, 94, 95, 144a]; post capt. in command of *Predpriatie* (*Enterprise*), 1824–1825, 1825. [96]

KRUSENSTERN, ADAM JOHN VON; Russian, author, capt. lieut. in

Russian navy, later an admiral; first Russian circumnavigator in command of *Nadeshda,* 1804, and *Neva,* Lisiansky, 1804. [97, 101, 110]

KUYKENDALL, RALPH S.; American, historian, author of a history of Hawaii and coauthor with Herbert E. Gregory of an earlier volume. These histories have been consulted for data not found in "historical narratives." [98, 98a]

La Bayonnaise; see *Bayonnaise.*

La Bonite; see *Bonite.*

La Boussole; see *Boussole.*

* *La Comète;* see *Comet.*

* *Lady Washington;* American registry, of Boston, brigantine (formerly a sloop), 90 tons, Capt. John Kendrick, master, 1791, 1794. [1, 84a, 98, 98a]

LAFOND, GABRIEL; French, author, on board *Alzire,* 1828. [99]

LA GRAVIÊRE, JURIEN DE; French, author, captain in French navy in command of *Bayonnaise,* 1850. [100]

* *L'Aigle;* see *Aigle.*

L'Alzire; see *Alzire.*

LAMBERT, CAPT. ——; ——, master of *Mary Dacre,* 1835. [175]

LANGLE, —— DE; French, post captain in French navy, with La Pérouse's expedition in command of *Astrolabe,* 1786. *See* La Pérouse.

LANGSDORFF, GEORGE HENRY VON; German, author, naturalist on *Nadeshda,* 1804. [101] *See also* Krusenstern.

LA PÉROUSE, JEAN FRANCOIS GALAUP DE; French, author, commodore in French navy in command of a voyage of discovery; *Boussole* and *Astrolabe,* de Langle, 1786. [102, 103, 104] The expedition was subsequently shipwrecked with no survivors.

LAPLACE, CYRILLE-PIERRE-THÉODORE; French, author, post captain in French navy, in command of *Artémise,* 1839. [105] Laplace's visit was one of avowed hostility. Under duress he forced the Hawaiian government to sign an unfair treaty and to pay $20,000 guaranty.

* *Lark;* American registry, ——, Capt. Northcop, master, 1813; Astor's third vessel, was wrecked off Kahoolawe; *see* Astor.

L'Artémise; see *Artémise.*

LA SALLE, A——— DE; French, author, probably not with Vaillant on *Bonite*, 1836. [106]   *See also* Vaillant.

La Solide; see *Solide.*

L'Astrolabe; see *Astrolabe.*

Lausanne; "from New York," ship, 500 tons, Capt. T. Spaulding, master; was here in April 1840 and again in December 1840. [2, 81, 109, 145]

LAUVERGNE, BARTHELME; French, artist with French government expedition, *Bonite*, 1836. [181a]

La Vénus; see *Vénus.*

La Ville de Bordeaux; see *Ville de Bordeaux.*

LAY, WILLIAM; American, coauthor with Cyrus Hussey; a seaman on *Globe*, 1823, *Dolphin*, 1826. [107]   See also *Globe.*

Le Bordelais; see *Bordelais.*

* LE BORGNE; French commander of *Sarcelle*, 1848. [71]

LEDYARD, JOHN; American, author, marine with Capt. Cook on *Resolution*, 1778, 1779. [108]   *See also* Cook, James.

Lee Boo; see *Prince Lee Boo.*

LEE, DANIEL; American, coauthor with J. H. Frost, Methodist missionary to Oregon; arrived *Ganymede*, 1835, departed *Nereid*, 1836; arrived *Diamond*, 1843, departed *Bhering*, 1843. [109]

LEE, S. S.; American, commander in U.S.N., in command of *Mississippi*, 1854. [71, 93]

* LEE, WILLIAM L.; American, arrived on *Henry*, October 12, 1846, Chas. R. Bishop, a fellow passenger. [71]   Lee became the first Chief Justice of the Supreme Court of the Hawaiian Islands.

Le Heros; see *Heros.*

Leland; American registry, merchant ship, T. Kellington, master, 1845. [71, 81]

Lelia Byrd; American registry, brig, 175 tons, William Shaler, master, 1803, 1805. *See* Cleveland, Richard, and Shaler.

LE NETREL, EDMOND; French, author, lieut. with Duhaut-Cilly on *Heros*, 1828. [109a]

Lewis; New Bedford registry, whaleship, Capt. Tollman, master, 1844. [45]

LEWIS, CAPT. ISAIAH; ————, master of *Panther*, 1817. [144a]

LISIANSKY, UREY; Russian, author, capt. lieut. in Russian navy under Krusenstern, in command of *Neva*, 1804. [110]   *See also* Krusenstern.

LITTLE, GEORGE; American, author, seaman; *Dromo*, 1809. [111]

LONG, A. K.; American, lieut. in command of *Relief*, 1839. *See* Wilkes.

LONG, J. C.; American, commander in U.S. Navy in command of *Boston*, 1843; commodore in command of *Merrimac*, 1858. [71, 74a]

LOOMIS, MARIA THERESA S.; American, author, wife of Elisha Loomis, printer; arrived with pioneer company of missionaries on *Thaddeus*, 1820. [112]

* *Loudoun;* see *Imperial Eagle.*

Louise; see *Princess Louise.*

LOW, CHARLES P.; American, author, in trade to China, master of *Samuel Russel*, 1850, and of *N. B. Palmer*, 1854. [71, 113]

LUCATT, EDWARD; British, author, merchant, *Mary*, 1849. [114]

L'Uranie; see *Uranie.*

LYMAN, ALBERT; American, merchant, author, seaman aboard the *Samuel Roberts*, 1850. [114a]

LYMAN, CHESTER SMITH; American, author, traveled for his health, "some time professor of Astronomy and Physics in Yale University"; arrived on *Mariposa*, 1846, left on *Euphemia*, 1847. [115]

LYMAN, SARAH JOINER; American, author, missionary teacher, wife of Rev. David Belden Lyman. Arrived with fifth company of American missionaries on *Averick*, 1832. [115a]

M'CLURE, ROBERT LE MESURIER; British, commander in British navy, in command of *Investigator*, 1850; while in search of *Erebus* and *Terror* under Franklin, made the Northwest Passage. [8, 139]

McKAY, CAPT. _____; American, master of *Sovereign of the Seas*, 1853. [14, 71]

MACRAE, JAMES; Scotsman, author, botanist with Lord Byron, *Blonde*, 1825. [116]

* MAGEE, CAPT. JAMES; co-owner and master of *Margaret*, 1792. [84, 84a]

* MAIGRET, LOUIS D.; _____, Catholic pro-vicar, arrived on *Europa*, November 1837, left on *Our Lady of Peace*, 1837; arrived on *Clementine*, 1840. [1, 98, 98a, 158]

74

* MALLET, CAPT. ———; French, captain in French navy, in command of *Embuscade*, 1842. Mallet made certain demands but when informed of Hawaiian embassy sent to France to ask for a new treaty, he left without pressing them further. [1, 98, 98a]

MANBY, THOMAS; British, author, master's mate with Vancouver's expedition; on *Discovery*, 1792, on *Chatham*, 1793, 1794. [116a]

MARCHAND, ÉTIENNE; French, made investigation of fur trade on northwest coast of America, in command of *Solide*, 1791. [68]

Margaret; British registry, ship, John Buyers, master, 1802–1803. [176]

* *Margaret;* American registry, 150 tons, Capt. James Magee, master, 1792. [84, 84a] *See also* "The Ship *Margaret . . .*" by F. W. Howay in *Thirty-eighth Annual Report of The Hawaiian Historical Society for the Year 1929.*

Maria; see *Wilhelmina en Maria.*

MARINER, WILLIAM; British, clerk, *Port au Prince*, 1806. [117]

Mariposa; American registry, merchant ship, 330 tons, Capt. Spalding, master, 1846. [115]

* *Maro;* Nantucket registry, Capt. Joseph Allen, master, 1820; first whaler to enter Honolulu harbor. *See* Thrum's *Hawaiian Annual* for 1909, p. 133.

* MARSHALL, J. F. B.; ———, secret envoy of king, 1843. See *Albert.*

MARTIN, JOHN; British, author of account of William Mariner's travels; did not visit Hawaii. [117]

Mary; "under protectorate flag," i.e., French, bark, Fleury, master, 1849. [114]

Mary Dacre; ——— registry, brig, Capt. Lambert, master, 1835. [175]

Mary Dare; British brig, 149 tons, belonged to Hudson Bay Co., Mount, master, 1851. [38, 145]

Mary Frazier; Boston registry, bark, 288 tons, Capt. Charles Sumner, master; brought eighth company of American missionaries, 1837. [129, 158, 188a]

Maryland; "from New York," ship, a trader, Jonathan Perry, Jr., master, 1807. [89, 141]

Maryland; American registry, brig, Capt. Couch, master, 1840. [2, 145] The *Maryland* on which Richard Charlton departed in 1842 possibly may be this same vessel.

Massachusetts; U.S. transport, sailing steamer, 750 tons, Capt. Wood, master, 1849. [169a] Second steam vessel to visit Hawaii.

MASSET, STEPHEN C.; ———, author, traveler; arrived on *Emeline,* 1850, left on *Odd Fellow,* 1850. [118] The date is an arbitrary one fixed after careful reading of the text.

Mastiff; ——— registry, clipper ship, Capt. Johnson, master, 1859. [71] *See also* Dana.

MATHISON, GILBERT FARQUHAR; British, author and traveler, *America,* 1822. [119]

MAY, CAPT. JOHN; English, master of ship *Japan,* 1832. [89a]

MAYNE, RICHARD CHARLES; British, author, lieut. in British navy on *Plumper,* 1857. [120]

Mazeppa; ——— registry, "clipper-built ship of 170 tons," ———, master, 1850. [161]

MEARES, JOHN; British, author, made "voyages of commerce," master of *Nootka,* 1787 and of *Felice,* 1788. *Iphigenia,* William Douglas, master, 1788–1789, 1789, was one of Meares' vessels. *North West America,* Robert Funter, master, accompanied the *Iphigenia* on her first visit to Hawaii. [121, 122, 123]

MEEK, CAPT. ———; ———, master of *Chinchilla,* 1832. [137]

MEEK, CAPT. JOHN; American, master of *Tamaahmaah,* 1824. [12a, 84a]

MELVILLE, HERMAN; American, famous as author of *Typee* and other books; left as a seaman on *United States,* 1843. [2a, 70]

MELVIN, JOHN L.; ———, author, seaman, first visit—*Argentina,* 1818; second visit—arrived on *Belgrano,* 1823, left on *Foster,* 1823; third visit—arrived on *Foster,* 1823, left on *Paragon,* 1823. [124]

* *Mentor;* "from New London," ship, Capt. Rice, master, brought sixth company of American missionaries, 1833. [129]

Mentor; American ship "of Boston," trader, Lemuel Porter, master and one of the owners, 1821. [81a, 84a] *Mentor* visited Hawaii on her first voyage to the Northwest Coast, 1818, Capt. John Suter, master, and made later visits to Hawaii.

MENZIES, ARCHIBALD; Scotsman, author, surgeon and naturalist; first visit—*Prince of Wales*, 1787–1788; *see* Colnett; second visit—*Discovery*, 1792, 1793, 1794. [125] *See also* Vancouver.

Mercury; British registry, brig, 152 tons, Capt. Cox, master, 1789. [131]

* *Mercury*; "of New Providence," snow, Capt. Barnett, 1795. [84]

Mermaid; British registry, sloop, 61 tons, Capt. Kent, master, 1822. [60, 61, 177]

Merrimac; U.S.N. steam frigate, Commodore John C. Long in command, 1858. [74a]

* METCALF, SIMON; American, trader, master of *Eleanora*, 1790. His son, Thomas, commanded the tender *Fair American*, 1790. By ordering the Olowalu Massacre, Simon Metcalf provoked the natives to retaliation. This the Hawaiians accomplished by capturing the *Fair American* and killing all the crew except Isaac Davis. When John Young, the boatswain, was sent ashore from the *Eleanora* a few days later, he was held by the natives for fear he would tell Metcalf of the fate of the crew of the *Fair American*. Young and Davis became two of Kamehameha I's chief advisors. For a discussion of Metcalf, *see* "Captain Simon Metcalfe and the Brig *Eleanora*" by Judge F. W. Howay in *Thirty-fourth Annual Report of The Hawaiian Historical Society for the Year 1925*.

* METCALF, THOMAS; American, master of *Fair American*, 1790; killed by natives; *see* Metcalf, Simon.

MEYEN, F. J. F.; Prussian, author, physician and naturalist, *Princess Louise*, 1831. [126, 127]

MEYERS, WILLIAM H.; American, author and artist, gunner on *Cyane*, 1843. [2a, 127a]

* MILLER, WILLIAM; British, arrived on *Hazard*, 1844, as consul-general for Great Britain. [1, 71]

Millwood; "from New York," ship, Samuel G. Bailey, master, 1815–1816. [12]

Milwaukee; American ship, ——, Capt. Rhoades, 1859. [190a]

Missionary Packet; American registry, schooner, 40 tons, James Hunnewell, master, 1826. Intended for use between the islands by the American missionaries. [86]   For a history

of the vessel, *see* "The Schooner *Missionary Packet*" by Ralph S. Kuykendall in *Forty-first Annual Report of The Hawaiian Historical Society for the Year 1932*, p. 81–90.

Mississippi; U.S. steam frigate, Commander S. S. Lee in command, 1854. [71, 93]

MONTGOMERY, JOHN B.; American, commander U.S.N., in command of *Portsmouth*, 1845. [71, 192]

* *Montreal;* American registry, ship, Capt. Snow, master, 1845. [71]

* MOORE, CAPT. ———; ———, master of *Phoenix*, 1794. [84]

MOORE, SAMUEL G.; American, master of *Morning Star*, 1857. See *Morning Star.*

MOORE, T. E. L.; British, commander in British navy, in command of *Plover*, 1848, in search of *Erebus* and *Terror*. [83]

Morning Star; American missionary packet, about 150 tons, Capt. Samuel G. Moore, master; carried supplies to missions in Micronesia; arrived at Honolulu on first visit April 24, 1857. This and three subsequent vessels financed by Sunday School children in United States and Hawaii. [21, 71, 184]

MORRELL, BENJAMIN, JR.; American, author, fur trader, master of *Tartar*, 1825. [130]

MORRIS, JAMES; Irish, clerk; his account is the basis of the book on the voyage of the *Arrow*, 1822. [182]

MORTIMER, GEORGE; British, author, lieut. of the marines, *Mercury*, 1789. [131]

MULLET, J. C.; British, author, seaman; first visit—*George and Susan*, 1849; mentions two other visits but gives no dates. [132]

MURAGAKI AWAJI-NO-KAMI; Japanese, author, second ambassador of the first Japanese embassy to the United States; *Powhatan*, 1860. [90a, 132a, 192a]

* MURPHY, JAMES C.; Irish, Catholic catechist, arrived *Europa*, November 1837. [1, 158]

MURRELL, WILLIAM MEACHAM; American, author, one of crew on *Columbia*, 1839. [133]

MYERS, JOHN; British, author; first visit—shipped on *Jane*, 1795 second visit—first officer on *Betsy*, 1800; third visit—on *Ann* 1802. [134]

Myrtle or *Kodiak;* see Scheffer.

Nadeshda; "Russian imperial service," ship, 450 tons, Capt. Lieut. Adam John von Krusenstern in command, 1804. [97, 101, 110]

N. B. Palmer; American registry, clipper ship, Charles P. Low, master, 1854. [71, 113]

Neptune; American registry, sealing ship, 350 tons, Daniel Greene, master, 1798. [174]

Nereid; bark owned by Hudson Bay Co., Capt. Royal, master, 1836. [109]

Neva; "Russian imperial service," ship, 350 tons, Lisiansky in command, 1804 [97, 110]; Hagemeister in command, 1809. [30, 97, 110]

NEVENS, WILLIAM; American, author, ship keeper, *Rosellic*, March and fall of 1826, March and September of 1827; *Hobomok*, 1835; *The Boy*, 1837. [135]

NEWELL, CAPT. FISHER AMES; American, brother of Capt. George Newell, first arrived Honolulu 1846 when he brought the royal yacht *Kamehameha III* from Boston. Resided in Honolulu for a number of years; master of *Honolulu*, 1849. [1, 71, 98, 135a]

NEWELL, CAPT. GEORGE; American, author, master of *Sea Breeze*, 1850. [135a]

* *New England;* "from New Bedford," ship, Capt. Parker, master; brought fourth company of American missionaries, 1831. [129]

New Hazard; Salem registry, brig, Capt. David Nye, Jr., master, 1811, 1812, 1813. [149a]

NICOL, JOHN; Scotsman, author, cooper and steward with Portlock on *King George*, 1786, 1786–1787, 1787. [136] *See also* Portlock.

* *Noble;* American registry, brig, 207 tons, Capt. Robertson, 1850. [145]

Nootka; British registry, 200 tons, John Meares, master, 1787. *See* Meares.

North America; American registry, bark, whaler, Capt. Richards, master, 1840. [138]

* NORTHCOP, CAPT. ——; ——, master of *Lark*, 1813. *See* Astor.

North West America; British registry, schooner, 40 tons, Robert Funter, master; "first vessel ever built in that part of the world"—i.e., northwest coast of America; accompanied *Iphigenia*, Wm. Douglas, master, to Sandwich Islands 1788–1789. *See* Meares.

NORTON, THOMAS HOWES; American, master of *Citizen*, 1852. [82]

NYE, CAPT. DAVID, JR.; American, master of *New Hazard*, 1811, 1812, 1813; described as brutal master. [149a]

O'Cain; Boston registry, 280-ton ship, trader, Capt. Jonathan Winship, master, 1806, 1813. [9, 84a, 141, 149a]   This vessel was a frequent visitor to Hawaii.

Odd Fellow; ——— registry, schooner, ———, master, 1850. [118]

Old Ironsides; see *Constitution.*

OLIVER, JAMES; American, author, seaman, first visit—*Glide*, 1830; second visit—arrived on *Chinchilla*, 1832, left on *Potomac*, 1832. [137]

OLMSTED, FRANCIS ALLYN; American, author, traveled for his health, arrived *North America*, 1840, left *Flora*, 1840. [138]

Ontario; American registry, whaling ship, Alex. D. Bunker, master, 1825, March 1826, September 1826. [29]

Ophelia; American registry, ship, about 360 tons, Samuel Hill, master and supercargo, 1816. [80a]

Oregon; U.S.N. brig, Lieut. Overton Carr, Wilkes Exploring Expedition, replacing *Peacock*, 1841. *See* Wilkes.

OSBORN, SHERARD; British, author of account of *Investigator's* voyage, 1850; did not visit Hawaii. [139]

Osprey; "ship, Brown, of Salem, from a sealing voyage"; 1818. James Hunnewell left on *Osprey*. [85]

Otkrytie or *Discovery;* see Scheffer.

Otter; Boston registry, three masts, Ebenezer Dorr, master, 1796–1797. [144]   *See also* Péron.

* *Our Lady of Peace;* ——— registry, schooner, formerly the *Missionary Packet*, bought by Catholics so Maigret and Bachelot might depart, 1837. [1, 98, 98a]

Owhyhee; Boston-owned brig, 116 (or 166?) tons, trader, left Honolulu for Boston via Canton, late 1827. [12a]

Packet; see *Bordeaux Packet, Missionary Packet.*

Palmer; see *John Palmer, N. B. Palmer.*

Panther; American brig, Capt. Isaiah Lewis, master, 1817. Dr. Georg Anton Scheffer left Hawaii aboard the *Panther*. [144a]

Paragon; American registry, ship, William Cole, master, 1823–

1824. [27]   John L. Melvin [124] speaks of leaving on the *Paragon* in November 1823. This may be the same vessel that Brewer came on.

* PARKER, CAPT. ———; ———, master of *New England*, 1831. [129]

PARKER, REV. SAMUEL; American, author, sent by A.B.C.F.M. on an exploring tour beyond the Rocky Mts.; returned home by way of Sandwich Islands, arriving here on *Columbia*, 1836, and departing on *Phoenix*, 1836. [140]

Parthian; American registry, merchant ship, 337 tons, Richard D. Blinn, master; brought third company of American missionaries, 1828. [78, 91, 92]

PATTERSON, SAMUEL; American, author, seaman; first visit—arrived on *Yarmouth*, 1805, left on *Hamilton*, 1806; second visit— arrived on *Pearl*, 1806, left on *O'Cain*, 1806; third visit— arrived on *Tamana*, 1807, left on *Maryland*, 1807. [141]

PATY, CAPT. JOHN; ———, master of *Don Quixote*, 1840. [66, 67]

PAULDING, HIRAM; American, author, lieut. U.S.N., *Dolphin*, 1826. [142]   *See also* Percival.

* PAULET, LORD GEORGE; British, captain in British navy, in command of *Carysfort*, 1843. Provisional cession of Hawaii to Great Britain, February 25, 1843, followed acts of Lord Paulet supporting machinations of Richard Charlton, British consul. Rear Admiral Richard Thomas restored the Hawaiian flag July 31, 1843. [1, 71, 92, 98, 98a]

* *Peacock;* U.S. sloop of war, Capt. Thomas ap Catesby Jones in command, 1826. *See* Jones.

Peacock; U.S. naval ship, 600 tons, Commodore Edmund P. Kennedy in command, 1836. [156, 158]

Peacock; U.S.N. sloop of war, 650 tons, Capt. William L. Hudson, Wilkes Exploring Expedition, 1840. Wrecked July 18, 1840 at mouth of Columbia River. *See* Wilkes.

PEALE, T. R.; American, naturalist and artist with Wilkes Exploring Expedition, 1840–1841. [189]

Pearl; Boston registry, 200 tons, Capt. John Ebbets, master, and John Suter, first mate, 1805, 1806. John Suter, master, 1808. [84e, 141]
    The *Pearl* made other voyages to Hawaii.

Pearl; H.B.M. screw steamship, 21-gun corvette, Capt. Sotheby in command, 1857, on duty in Pacific. [190]

PEARSON, CAPT. GEORGE F.; American naval officer in command of *Powhatan,* 1860. [90a, 132a, 192a]

* PEIRCE, HENRY AUGUSTUS; American, ship captain and merchant, associated with James Hunnewell and Charles Brewer; master of *Peru,* 1837. [1, 27, 89b, 98a, 158]

PERCIVAL, JOHN; American, U.S.N., lieut. in command of *Dolphin,* 1826, in pursuit of the mutineers of the *Globe.* [107, 142] Captain in command of *Constitution,* 1845. [71, 167] The behavior of Percival and his men in 1826 resulted in an investigation by a Naval Court of Inquiry which exonerated Percival.

The John Percival of the *Dolphin* is assumed to be the same person as the John Percival of the *Constitution.*

PERKINS, EDWARD T.; American, author, seaman, arrived *Planet,* 1849, staying twenty months, left _____. [143]

PÉRON, _____; French, author, his vessel, *Émilie,* captured by English; by giving his pelts as security, he obtained position of first officer on *Otter,* Ebenezer Dorr, visited Hawaii, 1796–1797. [144]

PÉROUSE; *see* La Pérouse.

* PERRIN, EMILE; French commissioner; first visit—arrived on *Virginie,* 1846, bringing new treaties; second visit—arrived on *Serieuse,* 1850, again presenting identical demands made by France in 1849 through Tromelin and Dillon. [1, 71]

PERRY, JONATHAN, JR.; American, master of *Maryland,* 1807. [89, 141]

Perseverance; American registry, 200 tons, Amasa Delano, master, 1801, 1806. [51]

* *Peru;* American registry, brig, chartered by Honolulu merchants Peirce and Brewer, Capt. G. E. Kilham, master, 1837. [89b, 98a, 158]

PETIT-THOUARS; *see* Du Petit-Thouars.

* *Phoenix;* _____ registry, Capt. Moore, master, 1794. [84]

Phoenix; "from New London," ship, 410 tons, Capt. Allyn, master, 1836. [140]

Planet; American registry, whaler, Capt. Peter Smith Buck, master, 1849. [143]

* PLASSARD, CAPT. _____; French, master of *Comet*, which brought the first Catholic missionaries, 1827. [1, 98, 98a]

Plover; H.B.M. bark, Commander T. E. L. Moore in command, 1848, in search of the *Erebus* and *Terror* under Franklin. [83]

PLUM, AUGUST; Danish, artist with Steen Anderson Bille on *Galathea*, 1846. [152]

Plumper; H.M.S. steam-sloop, Capt. George Henry Richards in command, sent to survey Vancouver Island and adjacent coast, 1857. [120]

Porpoise; U.S.N. brig, 230 tons, Lieut. Cadwalader Ringgold, Wilkes Exploring Expedition; arrived October 1840, on cruise to Paumotus from November through March, left in April 1841 for Northwest Coast, returning in November on way to China. *See* Wilkes.

Port au Prince; "private ship of war, belonging to Mr. Robert Bent, of London," 500 tons, Mr. Brown, master, 1806. [117]

PORTER, DAVID; American, author, capt. in U.S. Navy and superior officer of Lieut. John Gamble. [146]

PORTER, CAPT. LEMUEL; American, trader, master of *Hamilton*, 1806; co-owner and master of *Mentor*, 1821. [81a, 84a, 141]

PORTLOCK, NATHANIEL; British, author, with Cook on his last voyage, 1778, 1778–1789; headed expedition sent out by "*The King George's Sound Company* for carrying on a fur trade from the West Coast of America to China"; in command of *King George*, 1786, 1786–1787, 1787. [136, 147]   George Dixon on *Queen Charlotte* under Portlock. [53]

Portsmouth; U.S. Navy ship, _____, Commander John B. Montgomery, 1845. [71, 192]

POST, CAPT. _____; _____, master of *Huntress*, 1833, 1834. [173]

Potomac; U.S.N. frigate, Commodore John Downes in command, 1832. [137, 149, 186]

* *Poursuivante;* French naval frigate, Admiral de Tromelin in command, 1849. [1, 71]

Powhatan; U.S. Navy steam frigate, flagship of the East India Squadron, 2,415 tons, Capt. George F. Pearson in command, 1860. [90a, 132a, 192a]

Predpriatie or *Enterprise;* Russian Imperial Navy, frigate, Post Capt. Otto von Kotzebue in command, 1824–1825, 1825. [96]

* *Prince Lee Boo;* English registry, sloop, trader, Capt. Gordon, master, 1794. *See* Brown, William.

Prince of Wales; British registry, ship, 171 tons, trader, companion vessel to *Princess Royal;* Capt. James Colnett, master, 1788. [40a]   *See also* Colnett.

Prince Regent; ———— registry, schooner, 70 tons, built at Port Jackson, New South Wales; a present to Kamehameha II from King of England to fulfill a promise made to Kamehameha I by Vancouver, 1822. [60, 61, 177]

Princess Louise; Prussian registry, Capt. Wendt in command, 1831. [126, 127]   Third Prussian vessel to circumnavigate the globe.

Princess Royal; British registry, sloop, 65 tons, trader, Charles Duncan, master, 1788. With *Prince of Wales,* captured by the Spaniards, 1789. Sailed to Manila via Hawaii, by Manuel Quimper, master, 1791, to be returned to the English owners. [40a, 148a]

Providence; H.B.M. sloop of war, 400 tons, Capt. William Robert Broughton, January 1796, July 1796. [28]

Providence; French registry, schooner, Capt. Mitchell, master, 1847. [71]

PUGET, PETER; British, lieut. in British navy, in command under Vancouver of *Chatham* on her second and third visits, 1793, 1794. *See* Vancouver.

QUARTER MASTER, OLD; pseudonym of John Bechervaise, British, author, first class petty officer on B————m, 1826, 1827. [148]   The vessel was probably the *Blossom,* Capt. F. W. Beechey.

Queen Charlotte; British registry, 200 tons, Capt. George Dixon in command, 1786, 1787. *See* Portlock.

QUIMPER BENITEZ DEL PINO, MANUEL; Spanish, lieut.-of-frigate in Spanish navy, author, master of *Princess Royal,* 1791. [148a]   *See also* Colnett.

Raccoon; British sloop of war, Capt. Wm. Black, master, 1814. [86a]

RANDOLPH, EDWARD F.; American, master of whaleship *South Boston,* 1855. [58a]

READ, GEORGE C.; American, commodore in U.S. Navy, in command of *Columbia* and *John Adams,* Wyman, 1839. Read's visit helped to ease the tension caused by Laplace of the *Artémise*. [18, 133, 170]

Regent; see *Prince Regent.*

Relief; U.S.N. store ship with Wilkes Exploring Expedition, "sent home from Callao by way of Sandwich Islands and Sydney," 1839, Lieut. A. K. Long in command. *See* Wilkes.

Remorino; see *Jane Remorino.*

Resolution; H.B.M. sloop, 452 tons, Capt. James Cook's third voyage, commanded successively by Capt. Cook, Capt. Clerke, and Capt. Gore, 1778, 1779. *See* Cook, James.

Restless; American, schooner, passenger vessel, Capt. Brown, master, 1855; brought Charles Victor Crosnier de Varigny. [180a]

REYNOLDS, J. N.; American, author, private secretary to Commodore Downes, *Potomac,* 1832. [149]

REYNOLDS, STEPHEN; American, author, seaman; three visits on *New Hazard,* 1811, 1812. Fourth visit, 1813, arrived *Isabella,* left *New Hazard.* Came back 1822–1823, settled in Honolulu as merchant, lawyer, harbor master, and pilot. Returned to his native Massachusetts in 1855 and died in 1857. [149a]

RHOADES, CAPT. ———; ———, master of *Milwaukee,* 1859. [190a]

* RICE, CAPT. ———; ———, master of *Mentor,* 1833. [129]

RICHARDS, CAPT. ———; American, master of *North America,* 1840. [138]

RICHARDS, GEORGE HENRY; British, captain in British navy, in command of H.M.S. *Plumper,* 1857. [120]

* RICHARDS, WILLIAM; American, ordained missionary, arrived with second company on *Thames,* 1823 [168]; left mission to serve in Hawaiian government as Minister of Public Instruction, 1838; with Timothy Haalilio departed as envoy to foreign powers on *Shaw,* 1842, returning on *Montreal,* 1845. [1, 71, 98, 98a]

RICKMAN, JOHN; British, author, second lieut. in British navy, on Cook's third expedition, on *Discovery* and later on *Resolution,* 1778, 1779. [150] *See also* Cook, James.

RICORD, JOHN; American, Kamehameha III's first legal advisor; arrived from Oregon on *Columbia,* 1844, Gustavus Hines a fellow passenger. [81] Left for San Francisco on *Providence,* 1847. [71]

RINGGOLD, CADWALADER; American, lieut.-commandant, U.S.N., Wilkes Exploring Expedition, in command of *Porpoise*, 1840, 1841. *See* Wilkes.

* ROBERTS, CAPT. JOSIAH; ———, master of *Jefferson*, 1793, 1794. [84, 84a]

* ROBERTSON, CAPT. ———; ———, master of *Noble*, 1850. [145] *Robertson;* see *Samuel Robertson*.

ROBSON, ANTHONY; British, master of *Columbia*, January 1815. [46]

ROQUEFEUIL, M. CAMILLE DE; French, author, on a trading voyage to China, master of *Bordelais*, 1819. [151]

Rosellic; American registry, whaler, Capt. Gardner, master, March and fall of 1826, March and September 1827. [135]

ROSEN, W. VON; ———, author; wrote account of Steen Bille's voyage on *Galathea*, 1846. [152, 153]

ROSS, ALEXANDER; American, author, clerk in Astor's enterprise, *Beaver*, 1812. [154]   *See also* Astor.

* ROUCHOUSE, ÉTIENNE; ———, Catholic bishop of Nilopolis, arrived on *Clementine*, 1840, departed on ———, early 1841. [1, 98, 98a]

ROVING PRINTER; ———, author, on *Emily*, 1853. [155]

ROWAN, CAPT. JAMES; American, master of the *Eliza*, 1799. [84c]

Royal; see *Princess Royal*.

ROYAL, CAPT. ———; ———, master of *Columbia*, 1836. [175]

ROYAL, CAPT. ———; ———, master of *Nereid*, 1836. [109]

* *Ruby;* "of Bristol, England," 101 tons, Charles Bishop, master, 1795. [84]

RUGGLES, SAMUEL and wife NANCY; Americans, authors, missionary teachers; arrived with pioneer company of American missionaries on *Thaddeus*, 1820. [155a]

Rurick or *Rurik;* of the Russian Imperial Navy, brig, 180 tons, Lieut. Otto von Kotzebue in command; Adelbert von Chamisso, naturalist, Louis Choris, artist. [30a, 94, 95, 144a]

RUSCHENBERGER, DR. W. S. W.; ———, author, surgeon in U.S.N. on *Peacock*, 1836. [156]

Russell; American registry, ship, Capt. Coleman, master, 1824. Rev. Wm. Ellis departed on *Russell*. [129]

Russell; see *Samuel Russell*.

* RUSSELL, LORD EDWARD; British, in command of *Acteon*, 1836.

On November 16, he negotiated a treaty between Great Britain and the Sandwich Islands which defined the rights of British subjects. [1, 98a]

RUSSUM, THOMAS; ———, master of *Euphemia*, 1847. [115]

* *Samoset;* "from Boston," ship, Capt. Hollis, master, brought twelfth company of American missionaries, 1848. [71]

Samuel Roberts; American schooner, Charles A. Falkenberg, master, 1850; purchased in California in 1849 by Connecticut Mining and Trading Co. [114a]

Samuel Robertson; "of Fairhaven," whaleship, Capt. Turner, master, 1848. [188]

Samuel Russell; American registry, ship, 92 tons, Charles P. Low, master, 1850. [71, 113]

SAMWELL, DAVID; Welsh, author, with Cook's third expedition, surgeon of the *Discovery*, 1778, 1779. [44, 44a, 157]

Santa Rosa; "American built, about 300 tons." A pirate ship under Capt. Turner, she arrived in May 1818; bought by Kamehameha I but seized by *Argentina*, Bouchard, late in September 1818. Peter Corney, who commanded the *Santa Rosa* on her departure in October 1818, gives a full account of this episode in his book. [46]

* *Sarah Abigail;* "from Boston," brig, Capt. Doane, master, brought tenth company of American missionaries, 1842. [129]

Sarah and Elizabeth; British registry, whaler, Capt. Swain, 1832. [15]

* *Sarcelle;* French naval corvette; Le Borgne in command, 1848. [71]

Savannah; U.S. Navy ship; Capt. James Armstrong in command, 1844. [71, 192]   Commodore John D. Sloat in command, 1845. [71, 93]

S. B. Wheeler; American registry, steamer (sidewheeler), 114 tons, Capt. Gus Ellis, master, 1853; T. Robinson Warren a passenger. [71, 185]   Renamed *Akamai*, this was the first vessel owned by the Hawaiian Steam Navigation Co. *See also* "Pioneer Hawaiian Steamers 1852–1877" by John Haskell Kemble in *Fifty-third Annual Report of The Hawaiian Historical Society for the Year 1944.*

SCHEFFER (SHAFFER), DR. GEORG ANTON; German, physician, author, employed by the Russian-American Company as

87

ship's doctor and later as leader of the attempted Russian occupation, principally on Kauai. Arrived on *Isabella*, 1815, departed on *Panther*, 1817. [144a]   Other ships used by the Russians in this venture: *Otkrytie* (*Discovery*), *Kodiak* (*Myrtle*), *Ilmen*, and *Bering*. See also "The Proceedings of the Russians on Kauai, 1814–1816," by W. D. Alexander in *Papers of The Hawaiian Historical Society*, no. 6.

Sea Breeze; "from Boston," bark, Capt. George Newell, master, 1850. [135a]

SEEMANN, BERTHOLD; German, author, botanist, *Herald*, 1849, 1850. [159]

* *Serieuse;* French naval corvette, ———, commander, 1850. *See* Perrin.

* SEYMOUR, CAPT. ———; ———, master of *Garafilia*, 1836. [158] *See also* Walsh.

SEYMOUR, SIR GEORGE F.; British, rear admiral in British navy, in command of *Collingwood*, 1846. [71, 183]

SHAFFER; *see* Scheffer.

SHALER, WILLIAM; American, author, trader, partner of Richard J. Cleveland, master of *Lelia Byrd*, 1803; brought first horse to Hawaii. On his second visit in 1805, the *Lelia Byrd* leaked so badly that Shaler exchanged her on September 9, 1805 for the *Tamana*, a schooner Kamehameha I was building. Shaler, placing John Hudson in command of the *Tamana*, left the islands on the *Atahualpa*, 1805. [160]   *See also* Cleveland, Richard.

* *Shaw;* ——— registry, schooner, ———, master, 1842. *See* Richards, William.

SHAW, CAPT. ———; ———, master of *Europa*, January 1837 and November 1837. [1, 158, 175]

SHAW, WILLIAM; British, author, in search of adventure, *Mazeppa*, 1850. [161]

* SHORT, PATRICK; ———, Catholic missionary, first visit—arrived on *Comet*, 1827, left on *Waverly*, 1831; second visit—arrived on *Clementine*, 1837, left on *Peru*, 1837. [1, 98, 98a, 158]

SHUBRICK, COM. ———; American, officer in U.S.N., in command of *Independence*, 1848. [71, 191]

* SIMPSON, ALEXANDER; British, bearer of dispatches to British Foreign Office, 1843. See *Albert*.

SPENCE, CAPT. ———; British, master of *Duke of Portland*, 1810. [30]

SPRING, CAPT. ———; American, master of *Flora*, 1840. [138]

Stanton; American registry, whaler, Capt. Howland, master, 1825, 1826. [20, 52]

* STARBUCK, CAPT. VALENTINE; ———, master of *Aigle*, 1823. See *Aigle*.

* *Starling;* Hawaiian schooner, Capt. Winckley, master, 1848. [89b, 145]

Starling; H.B.M. schooner, tender to *Sulphur*, Lieut. Henry Kellett in command under Capt. Edward Belcher, 1837, 1839. [17]

States; see *United States.*

STAVERS, T. R.; British, master of *Tuscan*, April 1834, October 1834, October 1835. [19]

Steiglitz; American registry, whaleship, Capt. Selah Young, master, 1845. [71, 165]

STEVENS, BENJAMIN; American, author, clerk for Capt. John Percival, *Constitution*, 1845. [167]

STEWART, CHARLES SAMUEL; American, author, missionary, arrived with second company on *Thames*, 1823; departed on *Fawn*, 1825 [168]; second visit, chaplain in U.S. Navy on *Vincennes*, 1829. [169]

STOCKTON, ROBERT F.; American, commodore U.S.N. in command of *Congress*, 1846. [41, 42, 71, 180]

STRIBLING, CORNELIUS K.; American, commander in U.S. Navy, in command of *Cyane*, 1843. [1, 71, 127a]

Sulphur; H.B.M. ship, 380 tons, Capt. Sir Edward Belcher in command, Richard Brinsley Hinds, surgeon, 1837, 1839; accompanied by *Starling*, Kellet. [17, 80b]

* SUMNER, CAPT. ———; ———, master of *Waverly*, 1831. [1, 98a]

SUMNER, CHARLES; American, master of *Mary Frazier*, 1837. [129, 158, 188a]

SUTER, CAPT. JOHN; American, first mate of *Pearl*, 1805, 1806 and may have been writer of the log. He was master of *Pearl*, 1808, of *Atahualpa*, 1812, 1813, of *Mentor*, 1818, of *Cleopatra's Barge*, 1820. [84a, 84b, 84e, 144a]

SWAIN, CAPT. ———; British, master of *Sarah and Elizabeth*, 1832. [15]

SWAIN, CAPT. EDWARD; ———, master of *Averick,* 1832. [31, 63, 115a]

SYKES, JOHN; British, master's mate and artist with Vancouver, *Discovery,* 1792, 1793, 1794. [178, 179]

Sylph; ———, brig, Capt. Alexander Adams, master; Peter Dobell, owner and passenger, 1819. [53a]

SYLVESTER, CAPT. AVERY; ———, master of *Chenamus,* 1845. [81]

TABULEVITCH; Russian aboard *Kamchatka;* drew chart of Honolulu harbor, 1818. [74b]

TALBOT, THEODORE; American, lieut. U.S. Army, author, *Massachusetts,* 1849. [169a]

Tamaahmaah; American brig, 240 tons, trader, Capt. John Meek, master, 1824. Sold in February 1828 to King Kamehameha III. [12a, 84a]

Tamana; —— —— registry, schooner, 45 tons, John Hudson, master, 1805, 1806; built at Hawaii. *See* Shaler, and Patterson.

Tartar; American registry, schooner, 154 tons, Capt. Benjamin Morrell, Jr., master, 1825. [130]

TATNALL, COMMODORE JOSIAH; American, flag officer of East India Squadron, U.S. Navy, *Powhatan,* 1860. [90a, 132a, 192a]

TAYLOR, CHARLES; ———, master of *Volunteer,* 1829. [77]

TAYLOR, FITCH W.; American, author, U.S. Navy chaplain, *Columbia,* 1839. [170]

TEN EYCK, ANTHONY; American, U.S. Commissioner to Hawaii, passenger on *Congress,* 1846. [180]

Terror; see *Erebus* and *Terror.*

Thaddeus; American registry, brig, 241 tons, Capt. Andrew Blanchard, master; brought pioneer company of American missionaries, 1820. [81a, 112, 129, 155a, 172] *See also* Hunnewell.

THAIN, JOHN MOUNT; ———, owner-captain of *Emily Bourne,* 1852. [111a]

Thames; American registry, ship, Capt. Clasby, master; brought second company of American missionaries, 1823. [168]

The Boy; American registry, whaler, 260 tons, Capt. Barton, master, 1837. [135]

THIERCELIN, ———; French, author and doctor; *Ville de Bordeaux,* 1839. [171]

* THOMAS, RICHARD; British, rear admiral in British navy, flagship *Dublin*, 1843. *See* Paulet.

THORN, CAPT. JONATHAN; American naval officer on leave, master of Astor's first vessel, *Tonquin*, 1811. [69, 69a]

THURSTON, LUCY GOODALE; American, author, wife of Rev. Asa Thurston, missionary, arrived with pioneer company on *Thaddeus*, 1820. [172]

TOLLMAN, CAPT. _____; _____, master of *Lewis*, 1844. [45]

Tonquin; American registry, ship, 300 tons, Capt. Jonathan Thorn, master, 1811; Astor's first vessel. [69, 69a, 154] *See also* Astor.

TORREY, WILLIAM; American, author, seaman, *Huntress*, 1833, 1834; _____, 1837. [173]

TOWNSEND, EBENEZER, JR.; American, author and supercargo, *Neptune*, 1798. [174]

TOWNSEND, JOHN K.; American, author, naturalist, member of an expedition of the Columbia River Fishing and Trading Co. to establish trading posts beyond Rocky Mts., headed by Capt. Wyeth; visited Hawaii on *Mary Dacre*, 1835, and arrived again on *Columbia*, 1836, leaving on *Europa*, 1837. [175]

* TROMELIN, LEGOARANT DE; French, rear admiral in French navy, in command of *Poursuivante*, 1849, conducted a series of "reprisals" after presenting ten demands drawn up by Dillon, French consul. [1, 71, 98a]

Tsar; American registry, merchant ship, 700 tons, Samuel Kenneday, master, 1848. [188]

TUCKER, CAPT. _____; British, in British navy in command of *Cherub*, 1814. [146] *See also* Gamble.

TURNBULL, JOHN; British, author, trader, part-owner with John Buyers; in charge of cargo and trade, *Margaret*, 1802–1803. [176]

TURNER, CAPT. _____; _____, in command of pirate vessel, *Santa Rosa*, 1818. [46]

TURNER, CAPT. _____; _____, master of *Samuel Robertson*, 1848. [188]

TURRILL, JOEL; American, U.S. consul-general at Honolulu, passenger on *Congress*, 1846. [180]

Tuscan; British registry, whaleship, 300 tons, T. R. Stavers, master, April 1834, October 1834, October 1835. [19]

TYERMAN, REV. DANIEL; British, coauthor with George Bennet, missionary, *Mermaid,* 1822. [177] *See also* Ellis, Rev. William.

TYLER, CAPT. ———; ———, master of *Isabella,* 1815. [144a]

Uncas; American registry, whaleship, Capt. Chas. W. Gelett, master, touched at Hawaiian Islands several times during whaling seasons of 1844 and 1845. [72]

Union; Boston registry, sloop, 89 tons, John Boit, Jr., master, 1795. [25]

United States; U.S. Navy frigate, Capt. James Armstrong in command, attached to U.S. Pacific Squadron under Commodore Thomas ap Catesby Jones, 1843. [2a, 70, 71]

Uranie; French registry, corvette, Capt. Louis de Freycinet in command on a French exploring and scientific expedition, 1819. Aboard were Capt. Freycinet's wife, Madame Rose de Freycinet, and Jacques Arago, draftsman. [4, 5, 6, 7, 70a, 70b]

VAILLANT, AUGUSTE NICOLAS; French, captain in French navy in command of *Bonite* on a government expedition, 1836. [13, 106, 181a] Obtained permission for Walsh, Irish priest, to remain in Hawaii.

Vancouver; ——— registry, ship, Capt. Duncan, master, 1839–1840. [66, 67, 98a]

VANCOUVER, GEORGE; British, author, in British navy, midshipman with Capt. Cook, 1778, 1779, *see* Cook, James; captain in command of *Discovery* and *Chatham,* Broughton, 1792, 1793, 1794; *Daedalus,* Hergest, 1792. [18a, 116a, 125, 178, 179]

VAN DENBURGH, MRS. ELIZABETH DOUGLAS TURRILL; American, author; when a young girl, accompanied her father, Joel Turrill, to Hawaii on *Congress,* 1846. [180]

VARIGNY, CHARLES VICTOR CROSNIER DE; French, author, arrived on *Restless,* 1855; departed *Montana,* 1868. [180a] In the 1860s, Varigny served in the cabinet of King Kamehameha V, first as Minister of Finance and later as Minister of Foreign Affairs.

VASSAR, JOHN GUY; American, author, traveled for his health, here in June through July 1851, vessel not found. [181]

Vénus; French naval frigate, Capt. Abel Du Petit-Thouars in command, 1837. [58]

* *Victoria;* Hawaiian schooner belonging to Kamehameha III, seized by Lord Paulet and sent in March 1843 to Valparaiso with dispatches for Admiral Thomas. [1, 71, 98, 98a]

Ville de Bordeaux; French registry, whaler, ———, master, 1839. [171]

Vincennes; U.S.N. corvette, Captain William Finch, 1829. [169]

Vincennes; U.S.N. sloop of war, 780 tons, Commodore Charles Wilkes, Wilkes Exploring Expedition, 1840, 1841. [34, 43, 64, 189]

VIRGIN, C. A.; Swedish, captain in Swedish navy, in command of *Eugenie,* 1852. [3, 71, 163, 163a] *Eugenie* was the first Swedish man-of-war to visit Hawaii.

* *Virginie;* French naval frigate, Rear Admiral Hamelin, 1846. [1, 71]

Volunteer; from Boston, bark, Capt. Charles Taylor, master, 1829. [77]

Wales; ——— registry, ship, ———, master, 1843. [32]

* WALKER, CAPT. ———; ———, master of *Clementine,* 1840. [145]

WALPOLE, THE HON. FRED; British, author, lieut. in British navy, *Collingwood,* 1846. [183]

* WALSH, ROBERT; Irish, Catholic priest, arrived on *Garafilia,* 1836. Because he was a British subject, Walsh was allowed to remain, provided he did not teach the Hawaiians, through the intervention of Capt. Vaillant of the *Bonite.* [1, 98, 98a]

WARREN, MRS. JANE S.; ———, author, wrote a history of *Morning Star.* [184]

WARREN, T. ROBINSON; ———, author, traveler; arrived on *Akamai,* formerly *S. B. Wheeler,* 1853; left "in a fine clipper ship," date not given. [71, 185]

WARRINER, FRANCIS; American, author, schoolmaster, *Potomac,* 1832. [186]

Washington; see *Lady Washington.*

* *Waverly;* ——— registry, brig, Capt. Sumner, master, 1831, took away the banished Catholic missionaries. [1, 98a]

WEBBER, JOHN; born in London, son of a Swiss sculptor; landscape painter, draftsman with Capt. James Cook. [44, 44a]

* *Wellington;* ship from San Blas, Mexico, ———, master; introduction of mosquitoes at Lahaina, 1826. [1]

WENDT, CAPT. ———; Prussian, in command of *Princess Louise,* 1831. [126, 127]

WESTON, CAPT. ———; ———, master of *Congaree,* 1844. [89b, 158]

WHEELER, DANIEL; British, author, minister of the Society of Friends, *Henry Freeling,* 1835–1836. [187]

Wheeler; see *Akamai.*

WHIDDEN, JOHN D.; American, author, seaman, arrived on *Tsar,* 1848, deserted at Honolulu, departed on *Samuel Robertson,* 1848. [188]

WHITE, CAPT. ———; ———, master of *George and Susan,* 1849. [132]

WHITE, DR. ELIJAH; American, Methodist missionary to Oregon, first visit—arrived *Hamilton,* 1836, left *Diana,* 1837; second visit—arrived *Maryland,* 1840, left *Lausanne,* 1840. [2]

WILCOX, ABNER and LUCY (HART); American, authors and missionary teachers; arrived with eighth company of American missionaries on the *Mary Frazier,* 1837. [188a]

WILDES, CAPT. DIXEY; American, master of *Atahualpa,* 1802. [11, 65]

Wilhelmina en Maria; Dutch registry, ship, in command of ———, 1828. [23] *See also* Boelen.

WILKES, CHARLES; American, author, commodore U.S. Navy, commander of U.S. Exploring Expedition, *Relief,* 1839; *Vincennes,* 1840–1841, 1841; *Peacock,* Hudson, 1840; *Porpoise,* Ringgold, 1840, 1841; *Flying Fish,* Knox, 1840; *Oregon,* Carr, 1841. [34, 43, 64, 189]

WILLIAMS, REV. EDWARD A.; British, author, British navy, chaplain on *Pearl,* 1857. [190]

WILLIAMSON, JOHN; British, author, lieut. with Cook's third expedition, 1778, 1779. [44a] *See also* Cook, James.

WILSON, W. F.; ———, editor of the diaries of David Douglas, of James Macrae, and of Archibald Menzies. [55, 116, 125]

WINCKLEY, CAPT. ———; ———, master of *Starling,* 1848. [89b, 158] It is possible this name is Hinckley.

WINSHIP, JONATHAN; American, trader, master of *O'Cain,* 1806,

1813. [9, 141, 149a]   He, with his brother Nathan Winship, did much to build up the early trade of Hawaii.

* WINSHIP, NATHAN; American, trader, master of *Albatross*, 1811, brother of Jonathan Winship.

WISE, HENRY AUGUSTUS; American, author, lieut. U.S.N., *Independence*, 1848. [191]

WOOD, CAPT. ———; American, master of U.S. transport *Massachusetts*, 1849. [169a]

WOOD, WM. MAXWELL, M. D.; American, author, surgeon, U.S.N., *Savannah*, 1844, *Portsmouth*, 1845. [192]   Wood's chapter on the Sandwich Islands indicates that the author came here twice, which fact was verified in *The Friend*. [71]

WORTH, THOMAS; American, master of *Globe*, 1823. See *Globe*.

* WYLLIE, ROBERT CRICHTON; Scotsman, arrived on *Hazard*, 1844, as secretary of William Miller, consul-general for Great Britain. [71]   Afterwards Wyllie became Minister of Foreign Affairs, 1845–1863. [1]

WYMAN, THOMAS; American, captain in U.S. Navy, in command under Commodore George C. Read of *John Adams*, 1839. See *Columbia*, U.S. frigate.

YANAGAWA MASAKIYO; Japanese, author, member of first Japanese embassy to America, *Powhatan*, 1860. [192a]

Yankee; American bark, passenger vessel, Capt. Hays, master, 1855. [58a]   Capt. Smith, master, 1857. [48a, 71]

Yarmouth; ——— registry, snow, ———, master, 1805. [141] This vessel had been secured at Sitka from the Russians as part payment for the *Juno*. Bancroft calls her the sloop *Ermak*. [9]

* YOUNG, JOHN; English, boatswain of *Eleanora*, 1790, became one of Kamehameha I's chief advisors. *See* Metcalf, Simon.

YOUNG, LEVI; American, master of *Harriet Blanchard*, 1830. [164]

YOUNG, SELAH; ———, master of *Steiglitz*, 1845. [71, 165]

ZIMMERMANN, HEINRICH; German, author, with Cook's third expedition, coxswain on *Discovery*, 1778, 1779. [193, 193a]   *See also* Cook, James.

1. ALEXANDER, W. D. *A Brief History of the Hawaiian People.*
   Published by order of the Board of Education of the Hawaiian Islands. New York: American Book Co. *c.* 1891.
   357 p.
   Numerous illustrations of Hawaii.

2. ALLEN, MISS A. J. (compiler). *Ten Years in Oregon. Travels
   and Adventures of Doctor E. White and Lady, ... with
   incidents of two sea voyages via Sandwich Islands around
   Cape Horn....* Ithaca, N. Y.: Andrus, Gauntlett, & Co.
   1850. 430 p.
   No illustrations.

2a. ANDERSON, CHARLES ROBERTS, ed. *Journal of a Cruise to the
   Pacific Ocean, 1842–1844, in the Frigate United States
   with Notes on Herman Melville....* Durham, N.C.: Duke
   University Press. 1937. 143 p.
   Three watercolors of Hawaii by William H. Meyers.

3. ANDERSSON, N. J. *Eene Reis om de Wereld met het
   Zweedsch oorlogsfregat Eugenie.* (1851–1853). Gronin-
   gen: J. B. Wolters. 1854. viii, 363 p.
   No illustrations.
   A typewritten copy of an English translation of the
   portion dealing with Hawaii is in the library.

4. ARAGO, JACQUES. *Narrative of a Voyage Round the World
   ... commanded by Captain Freycinet, during the years
   1817, 1818, 1819 and 1820....* London: Treuttel and
   Wurtz, Treuttel. 1823. 2 v. in 1.
   Six plates of Hawaii, one of *Uranie*, chart of voyage.

97

5. ARAGO, JACQUES. *Passeggiata Intorno al Mondo negli anni 1817–18–19 e 20 ... commandate dal sig. Freycinet....* Milan: Sonzogno. 1824. 4 v.

Three colored prints of Hawaii in vol. III.

6. ARAGO, M. JACQUES. *Souvenirs d'un Aveugle, Voyage Autour du Monde....* Third edition. Paris: Gayet et Lebrun. 1840. 4 v. in 2.

Eleven colored lithographs of Hawaii, portrait of Arago.

7. ARAGO, M. JACQUES. *Voyage Autour Du Monde.* Bruxelles: Société Typographique Belge. 1840. 570 p.

Eleven lithographs of Hawaii, portrait of Arago.

8. ARMSTRONG, ALEX. *A Personal Narrative of the Discovery North-west Passage....* London: Hurst and Blackett. 1857. xxii, 616 p.

One lithograph of *Investigator*, no illustrations of Hawaii.

9. BANCROFT, HUBERT HOWE. *History of Alaska.* 1730–1885. San Francisco: The History Co. 1890. 775 p.

No illustrations.

10. BANCROFT, HUBERT HOWE. *History of California.* Vol. II. 1801–1824. San Francisco: A. L. Bancroft & Co. 1885. xvi, 795 p.

No illustrations.

11. BANCROFT, HUBERT HOWE. *History of the Northwest Coast.* 1543–1846. San Francisco: A. L. Bancroft & Co. 1884. 2 v.

No illustrations.

12. BARNARD, CAPT. CHARLES H. *A Narrative of the Sufferings and Adventures ... during the years 1812 ... 1816....* New York: Printed for the author by J. Lindon, etc. 1829. 296 p.

No engravings of Hawaii, one of *Millwood.*

12a. BARRELL, GEORGE. *Notes on Voyages ... in a Career of Thirty Years at Sea....* Springfield, Ill.: H. W. Rokker. 1890. 223 p.

No illustrations.

13. BARROT, ADOLPHE. "Visit of the French Sloop of War Bonite, to the Sandwich Islands, in 1836," translation

from the French, in *The Friend,* vol. VIII, January through November 1850.

No illustrations.

13a. BARTLETT, JOHN. "A Narrative of Events ... in the years 1790–1793 ..." in *The Sea, The Ship and the Sailor.* Salem, Mass.: Marine Research Society. 1925.

Pen-and-ink sketch of the snow *Gustavus III.*

14. [BATES, GEORGE WASHINGTON]. *Sandwich Island Notes.* By a haole. New York: Harper & Brothers. 1854. 493 p.

Twenty-two engravings of Hawaii.

The London edition of 1854 is in the library.

15. BEALE, THOMAS. *The Natural History of the Sperm Whale ... to which is added a Sketch of a South-Sea Whaling Voyage.* London: John van Voorst. 1839. 12, 393 p.

One woodcut of Hawaii.

16. BEECHEY, CAPTAIN F. W. *Narrative of a Voyage to the Pacific ... performed in His Majesty's ship Blossom ... in the years 1825, 26, 27, 28.* Published by authority ... of the Admiralty. London: Henry Colburn and Richard Bentley. 1831. 2 v. in 1.

Chart of voyage, no illustrations of Hawaii.

Other editions are in the library.

17. BELCHER, SIR EDWARD. *Narrative of a Voyage Round the World, performed in Her Majesty's Ship Sulphur during the years 1836–1842. ...* Published under the authority ... of the Admiralty. London: Henry Colburn. 1843. 2 v.

One engraving of Hawaii, one chart of voyage.

18. [BELCHER, J. HENSHAW]. *Around the World: A narrative of a voyage in the East India Squadron, under Commodore George C. Read.* New York: Chas. S. Francis. 1840. 2 v.

No illustrations of Hawaii.

The 1847 edition, two vols. in one, is also in the library.

18a. BELL, EDWARD. "Log of the *Chatham"* [January 24, 1792 through February 26, 1794]," in *The Honolulu Mercury,* September 1929 through January 1930.

No illustrations.

19. BENNETT, FREDERICK DEBELL. *Narrative of a Whaling Voyage Round the Globe from the year 1833 to 1836. ...* London: Richard Bentley. 1840. 2 v.

No illustrations of Hawaii, chart of voyage.

19a. BILLE, STEEN ANDERSON. "Extract from Steen Bille's Report on the Voyage of the Danish corvette *Galathea* . . . in the years 1845–'46–'47," translated from the Danish by F. Banning, in *The Friend,* new series, vol. 12, January, March, and May 1863.

No illustrations.

20. BINGHAM, HIRAM. *A Residence of twenty-one years in the Sandwich Islands.* . . . First edition. Hartford: Huntington. 1847. 616 p.

Six engravings of Hawaii, portrait of Bingham.

21. BINGHAM, REV. HIRAM, JR. *Story of the Morning Stars, the Children's Missionary Vessels.* With sequels and a supplementary note. Boston: The American Board. 1907. 112 p.

Woodcuts of *Morning Stars.*

Pamphlets of earlier dates tell the story of the *Morning Star* more briefly.

22. BLOXAM, ANDREW. *Diary of Andrew Bloxam naturalist of the "Blonde" on her trip from England to the Hawaiian Islands 1824–25.* Bernice P. Bishop Museum Special Publication 10. Honolulu: Published by the Museum. 1925. 96 p.

Illustrated by photographs, portrait of Bloxam.

23. BOELEN, JACOBUS. *Reize naar de oost-en westkust van Zuid-Amerika . . . in de jaren 1826, 1827, 1828 en 1829. . . .* Amsterdam: Ten Brink & De Vries. 1835–1836. 3 v.

One engraving and one chart of Hawaii in vol. III; one chart of voyage in vol. I.

24. BOIT, JOHN, JR. "Remarks on the Ship Columbia's voyage from Boston (on a Voyage round the Globe)," in *Massachusetts Historical Society Proceedings,* vol. 53, p. 217–275. Boston: Published by the Society. 1920.

No illustrations.

25. BOIT, JOHN, JR. *The Journal of a Voyage Round the Globe* [on the Sloop *Union*]. Twenty-two photostat pages of portion dealing with Hawaii.

One photostat of drawing of *Union.*

26. BOLDUC, J.-B. Z. *Mission de la Columbie. Lettre et Journal*

de Mr. J.-B. Z. Bolduc, missionaire de la Colombie. Quebec: Fréchette. No date. 95 p.

No illustrations.

27. BREWER, CHARLES. *Reminiscences.* Jamaica Plain, 1884. 67 p.

No illustrations.

28. BROUGHTON, WILLIAM ROBERT. *A Voyage of Discovery to the North Pacific Ocean . . . performed in His Majesty's Sloop Providence, and her tender, in the years 1795, 1796, 1797, 1798.* London: Printed for T. Cadell and W. Davies. 1804. xx, 393 p.

No engravings of Hawaii.

The Weimar edition of 1805 is also in the library.

29. BUNKER, ALEX. D. *Log of the Whaling Ship Ontario.* Photostat of Hawaiian portion of Mss. 1825–1826 in Widener Library, Harvard University. 15 p.

No illustrations.

30. CAMPBELL, ARCHIBALD. *A Voyage Round the World, from 1806 to 1812.* . . . Edinburgh: Printed for Archibald Constable and Co. etc. 1816. 288 p.

No illustrations.

Other editions are in the library.

30a. CHAMISSO, ADELBERT VON. "Account of the Voyage Around the World on the *Rurik* 1815–1818" in *The Collected Works of Adelbert von Chamisso.* Leipzig. n.d. 4 v. Portion on Hawaii translated from the German by Victor S. K. Houston as "Chamisso in Hawaii," in *Forty-eighth Annual Report of The Hawaiian Historical Society for the Year 1939,* p. 55–82.

No illustrations.

31. CHAPIN, MARY ANN and DR. ALONZO. "Journal and Letters 1831–1833." Manuscript copy in four booklets.

No illustrations.

32. CHEEVER, REV. HENRY T. *The Island World of the Pacific: being . . . results of travel through the Sandwich or Hawaiian Islands.* . . . New York: Harper & Brothers. 1851. 406 p.

Eleven engravings of Hawaii, one map.

Four other editions are in the library.

33. CHORIS, LOUIS. *Voyage Pittoresque Autour Du Monde....* Paris: Firmin Didot. 1822. Folio with 110 plates.
    Nineteen lithographs of Hawaii.

34. CLARK, JOSEPH G. *Lights and Shadows of Sailor Life... including the more thrilling events of the U.S. Exploring Expedition....* Boston: John Putnam. 1847. 324 p.
    No illustrations.

35. CLEVELAND, H. W. S. *Voyages of a Merchant Navigator....* New York: Harper and Brothers. 1886. 245 p.
    Portrait of Richard J. Cleveland.

36. CLEVELAND, RICHARD J. *A Narrative of Voyages and Commercial Enterprises.* Second edition. Cambridge: John Owen. 1843. 2 v. in 1.
    No illustrations.
    Other editions are in the library.

37. COFFIN, GEORGE. *A Pioneer Voyage to California and Round the World—1849 to 1852....* Chicago, Ill.: Copyrighted by Gorham B. Coffin. 1908. 235 p.
    One reproduction of sketch of Honolulu.

38. COKE, HON. HENRY J. *A Ride Over the Rocky Mountains to Oregon and California....* London: Richard Bentley. 1852. x, 388 p.
    No illustrations of Hawaii, portrait of Coke.

39. COLLINSON, RICHARD. *Journal of H.M.S. Enterprise... in search of Sir John Franklin's ships... in 1850–55.* London: Sampson Low, Marston, Searle & Rivington. 1889. xii, 531 p.
    Portrait of Collinson, sketch of *Enterprise.*

40. COLNETT, JAMES. *A Voyage to the South Atlantic and Round Cape Horn into the Pacific Ocean... in the ship Rattler.* London: W. Bennett. 1798. xviii, 179 p.
    No illustrations of Hawaii.

40a. COLNETT, JAMES. "The Journal of ... aboard the Prince of Wales and Princess Royal from 16 Oct. 1786 to 7 Nov. 1788." Vol. 1. Original manuscript in British Public Record Office, London. Typed copy, gift of Mr. Donald Angus. 251 p.
    Original manuscript contains pencil sketches of Hawaii.

41. COLTON, REV. WALTER, U.S.N. *Deck and Port; or, incidents of a cruise in the United States frigate Congress....* New York: A. S. Barnes and Co. 1850. 408 p.
   Portrait of Commodore R. F. Stockton.

42. COLTON, REV. WALTER, U.S.N. *Deck and Port; or, incidents of a cruise in the United States frigate Congress....* Boston: Cleaves, Macdonald and Co. 1886. 408 p.
   One engraving of Hawaii.

43. COLVOCORESSES, GEORGE M. *Four Years in the Government Exploring Expedition; commanded by Capt. Charles Wilkes....* Fifth edition. New York: J. M. Fairchild & Co. 1855. 371 p.
   One woodcut of Hawaii.

44. COOK, JAMES, and KING, JAMES. *A Voyage to the Pacific Ocean...performed under the direction of Captains Cook, Clerke, and Gore, in his Majesty's ships the Resolution and Discovery in the years 1776, 1777, 1778, 1779, and 1780.* Vols. I and II by Cook, vol. III by King. Published by order...of the Admiralty. First Edition. London: Printed by W. and A. Strahan for G. Nichol and T. Cadell. 1784. 3 v. and atlas.
   In the atlas, twelve views of Hawaii by Webber, chart of Cook's discoveries. In vol. III, chart of the Sandwich Islands and of Kealakekua Bay.
   The third edition (London, 1785) also is present. There are many items in the library in several languages which are abridgments of earlier publications and also biographies: Kippis, Besant, Kitson, and others.

44a. COOK, JAMES. *The Journals of Captain James Cook....* Edited by John Cawte Beaglehole. Vol. III, parts 1 and 2. Cambridge University Press: for the Hakluyt Society. 1967. 1 v. in 2.
   Volumes I and II are not included because they do not contain information on Hawaii.
   Portraits of Cook, King, Gore, Clerke, Webber; silhouette of Samwell. Fifteen illustrations of Hawaii by John Webber, one possibly by William Ellis.
   ... *Charts and Views.* Edited by R. A. Skelton. 1955. Portfolio of 58 plates.
   Three charts of Hawaii.

103

45. Cook, John. *Reminiscences of John Cook Kamaaina and Forty-Niner.* Honolulu: The New Freedom Press. 1927. 27 p.

 No illustrations.

46. Corney, Peter. *Voyages in the Northern Pacific. Narrative of several trading voyages from 1813 to 1818, between the northwest coast of America, the Hawaiian Islands and China.* . . . Honolulu: Thos. G. Thrum. 1896. Reprinted from *The London Literary Gazette* of 1821. x, 138 p.

 No illustrations of Hawaii.

47. Cox, Ross. *Adventures on the Columbia River.* . . . London: Henry Colburn and Richard Bentley. 1831. 2 v.

 No illustrations.

 Other editions are in the library.

47a. Dampier, Robert. *To the Sandwich Islands on H.M.S. Blonde.* Edited by Pauline King Joerger. Honolulu: The University Press of Hawaii. 1971. 131 p.

 Twelve scenes of Hawaii, four portraits of Hawaiians, one self-portrait of Dampier.

48. Dana, Richard Henry, Jr. *Two Years Before the Mast.* . . . Boston: Houghton Mifflin Co. c. 1911. xiii, 553 p.

 No illustrations of Hawaii.

 The New York edition of 1840 is also in the library.

48a. Davies, Theophilus Harris. "Personal recollections of Hawaii." Written 1885; mimeographed c. 1959. 94 p.

 No illustrations.

49. Davis, R. C. *Reminiscences of a Voyage Around the World.* First edition. Ann Arbor, Michigan: Dr. Chase's Steam Printing House. 1869. 331 p.

 No illustrations.

50. Davis, William M. *Nimrod of the Sea; or, the American Whaleman.* New York: Harper and Brothers. 1874. 430 p.

 No engravings of Hawaii.

51. Delano, Amasa. *A Narrative of Voyages and Travels.* . . . Boston: E. G. House. 1817. 598 p.

 Portrait of Delano, no engravings of Hawaii.

52. Delano, Reuben. *Wanderings and Adventures of Reuben Delano, being a narrative of twelve years life in a whale*

ship! Worcester: Thomas Drew, Jr. 1846. 102 p.
  No engravings of Hawaii.

53. Dixon, Capt. George. *A Voyage Round the World . . . per-formed in 1785, 1786, 1787 and 1788. . . .* Second edition. London: George Goulding. 1789. xxix, 360, 47 p.
  Three engravings and two charts of Hawaii.
  The preface acknowledges that this account was written by Dixon's supercargo, Wm. Beresford.
  The French edition of 1789 is also in the library.

53a. Dobel, Pierre (Peter Dobell). *Sept Années en Chine, Nouvelles Observations sur cet Empire . . . et les Iles Sandwich.* Translated from the Russian by Le Prince Emmanuel Galitzin. Paris: Librarie d'Amyot. 1842. 358 p.
  No illustrations of Hawaii.

54. Dodge, George A. *A Narrative of a Whaling Voyage, in the Pacific Ocean, and its incidents.* Salem, Mass.: Press of the Salem Gazette. 1882. 30 p.
  No illustrations.

55. Douglas, David. *David Douglas, Botanist at Hawaii.* Edited by W. F. Wilson. Honolulu: The New Freedom Press. 1919. 83 p.
  Illustrations of Hawaii.

56. Douglas, David. *Journal Kept by David Douglas during his travels in North America 1823–1827 . . . with . . . an account of his death in 1834.* London: William Wesley & Son. 1914. 364 p.
  Portrait of Douglas.

57. Duhaut-Cilly, Auguste Bernard. *Viaggio Intorno Al Globo . . . negli anni 1826, 1827, 1828 e 1829. . . .* Translated from the French by Carlo Botta. Torino: Fontana. 1841. 2 v. in 1.
  One engraving of Hawaii.

58. Du Petit-Thouars, Abel. *Voyage Autour Du Monde sur la frégate La Vénus pendant les années 1836–1839. . . .* Paris: Gide, éditeur. 1840–1843. 4 v. in 2 and Atlas Pittoresque.
  The Atlas contains five lithographs of Hawaii.

58a. Egerstrom, Charles Axel. *Borta är Bra, Men Hemme är Bäst. . . . Färd Till Ostindien, Nord-Amerika, Kalifornien,*

Sandwichs-Öarna och Australien åren 1852–1857. . . . Stockholm: Albert Bonniers Forlag. 1859. 326 p.

No illustrations.

59. ELLIS, WILLIAM. *An Authentic Narrative of a Voyage performed by Captain Cook and Captain Clerke . . . during the years 1777, 1778, 1779, and 1780.* . . . First edition. London: Printed for G. Robinson, J. Sewell, and J. Debrett. 1782. 2 v.

Eight engravings of Hawaii.

The second edition (London, 1783) is also in the library.

60. ELLIS, WILLIAM. *Polynesian Researches, during a residence of nearly six years in the South Sea Islands.* . . . London: Fisher, Son & Jackson. 1829. 2 v.

No illustrations of Hawaii.

61. ELLIS, WILLIAM. *Polynesian Researches, during a residence of nearly eight years in the Society and Sandwich Islands.* Second edition, enlarged and improved. London: Fisher, Son & Jackson. 1831. 4 v.

Two engravings of Hawaii, one chart.

Later editions are in the library.

62. ELWES, ROBERT. *A Sketcher's Tour Round the World.* London: Hurst and Blackett. 1854. xii, 411 p.

Three colored lithographs of Hawaii from original drawings by the author.

63. EMERSON, OLIVER POMEROY. *Pioneer Days in Hawaii.* Garden City, N. Y.: Doubleday, Doran & Co. 1928. xiii, 257 p.

Many illustrations of Hawaii.

64. ERSKINE, CHARLES. *Twenty Years Before the Mast with . . . scenes and incidents while . . . under the command of . . . Charles Wilkes 1838–1842.* Philadelphia: George W. Jacobs and Co. 1896. x, 311 p.

Six illustrations of Hawaii; two portraits of author.

64a. "Extract from a pocket Diary by one of the officers of H.M.S. *Resolution,*" in *The Honolulu Mercury,* March 1930, p. 375–382.

No illustrations.

65. *Extracts from a Journal kept on board Ship Atahualpa,*

HOLMAN, LUCIA RUGGLES. *Journal.* . . . Bernice P. [
Museum Special Publication 17. Honolulu: 1931. 4
Portrait of author and her husband.

2. HOLMES, REV. LEWIS. *The Arctic Whaleman; or wi*
the Arctic Ocean. . . . Boston: Wentworth & Co.
296 p.
No illustrations of Hawaii.

83. HOOPER, W[ILLIAM] H[ULME]. *Ten Months Amor*
Tents of the Tuski. . . . London: John Murray. 18!
417 p.
No illustrations of Hawaii.

84. HOWAY, FREDERIC WILLIAM. "Early relations betwe
Hawaiian Islands and the Northwest Coast," i
Hawaiian Islands . . . Papers read during the C
Cook Sesquicentennial Celebration, Honolulu,
17, 1928. Albert P. Taylor and Ralph S. Kuyk
editors. Honolulu: Archives of Hawaii, Publicatic
5. 1930. 93 p.
No illustrations.

84a. HOWAY, FREDERIC WILLIAM. "A List of Trading
in the Maritime Fur Trade, 1795 . . . to . . . 1825," i
Transactions of the Royal Society of Canada, third
section II, vol. XXIV–XXVIII. 1930–1934.
No illustrations.

84b. HOWAY, FREDERIC WILLIAM. "Last Days of the *Atah*
alias *Bering*," in *Forty-first Annual Report of Th*
waiian Historical Society for the Year 1932.
No illustrations.

84c. HOWAY, FREDERIC WILLIAM. "The ship *Eliza* at Hav
1799," in *Forty-second Annual Report of The Hai*
Historical Society for the Year 1933, p. 103–113.
No illustrations.

84d. HOWAY, FREDERIC WILLIAM. "The *Caroline* and the
cock at Hawaii in 1799," in *Forty-fifth Annual Rep*
The Hawaiian Historical Society for the Year 19
25–29.
No illustrations.

84e. HOWAY, FREDERIC WILLIAM. "The Ship *Pearl* in H

bound on a Voyage from Boston to the N. W. Coast and
Sandwich Islands. Photostat of p. 242–245 of original in
Massachusetts Historical Collection, 1st series, vol. 9,
1804.
No illustrations.

66. FARNHAM, T. J. *Life, Adventures, and Travels in California.*
. . . Pictorial edition. New York: Nafis & Cornish, 1849.
468 p.
Five engravings of Hawaii.

67. FARNHAM, THOMAS J. *Travels in the Californias, and scenes*
in the Pacific Ocean. New York: Saxton & Miles. 1844.
96 p.
No illustrations.

68. FLEURIEU, C. P. CLARET. *A Voyage Round the World, per-*
formed during the years 1790, 1791 and 1792 by Étienne
Marchand. . . . Translated from the French of Fleurieu.
London: Printed for T. N. Longman, etc. 1801. 2 v.
No illustrations.

69. FRANCHERE, GABRIEL. *Narrative of a Voyage to the North-*
west Coast of America in the years 1811, 1812, 1813, and
1814. . . . Edited and translated from the original French
edition of 1820 by J. V. Huntington. New York: J. S.
Redfield. 1854. 376 p.
No engravings of Hawaii.
A reprint of this 1854 edition may be found in Reuben
Gold Thwaites: *Early Western Travels: 1748–1846,* vol.
VI, 1904.

69a. FRANCHERE, GABRIEL. *Adventure at Astoria, 1810–1814.*
Translated and edited by Hoyt C. Franchere. Norman,
Okla.: University of Oklahoma Press. 1967. xxxix, 190 p.
No illustrations of Hawaii; portrait of Franchere.

70. FRANKLIN, SAMUEL R. *Memories of a Rear-Admiral.* . . .
New York: Harper & Brothers. 1898. 398 p.
No illustrations of Hawaii, portrait of Franklin.

70a. FREYCINET, LOUIS DE. *Voyage Autour du Monde, . . . Exe-*
cuté sur les Corvettes de L. M. l'Uranie et la Physicienne,
pendant les années 1817, 1819 et 1820. . . . Vol. II. Paris:
Chez Pillett Aine. 1829.
No illustrations.

70b. FREYCINET, ROSE DE SAULCES DE. *Journal of....* Paris: Société d'Éditions Géographiques. 1927. 190 p.

> One watercolor of Hawaii.

> A portion of this journal, translated from the French by Victor S. K. Houston, was published in *Paradise of the Pacific,* November 1936 through April 1937.

71. *Friend, The.* A monthly paper edited by the Rev. S. C. Damon, D.D. Published since January 1843; bimonthly in 1845, 1846, 1847; suspended from May to September 1849 and from February 1851 to May 1852.

> Arrivals and departures of vessels are included in each issue. Narratives of voyages reprinted in *The Friend* are indexed separately in this volume.

72. GELETT, CHARLES WETHERBY. . . . *A Life on the Ocean autobiography of Captain Charles Wetherby Gelett.* Reprinted by permission from *The Ojai,* a California newspaper of the early 1890s. Honolulu: Hawaiian Gazette Co. 1917. 119 p.

> Portrait of Gelett.

73. GERSTAECKER, FREDRICH W. C. *Narrative of a Journey Round the World....* New York: Harper & Brothers. 1855. 624 p.

> No illustrations.

74. GILBERT, GEORGE. *The Death of Captain James Cook.* Hawaiian Historical Society Reprints, No. 5. Honolulu. 1926. 30 p.

> No illustrations.

74a. GILMAN, WILLIAM HENRY. *Letters . . . while acting as secretary to Commodore John C. Long, commander of the U.S. Steam frigate Merrimac . . . 1857–1858.* Exeter, N.H. 1911. 96 p.

> Portraits of Long and Gilman.

74b. GOLOVNIN, VASILII MIKHAILOVICH. *Puteshestvie Vokrug' Svieta, po Povelieniiu Gosudaria Imperatora Sovershennoe, na Voennom' Shliupie Kamchatkie v' 1817, 1818 i 1819 Godakh', Flota Kapitanom' Golovniniem'.* Saint Petersburg: V Morskoi Tipografii. 1822. 2 v.

> Chart of Honolulu harbor by Tabulevitch, 1818.

75. GOLOVNIN, VASILII MIKHAILOVICH. "Golovnin's Visit to Ha-

waii in 1818," translation by ... from tenth and eleventh cha... *Around the World....* St. Pet... *Friend,* vol. LII, July and August...

> No illustrations.

76. GRAHAM, MRS. MARIA, compiler. *Voy... Blonde to the Sandwich Islands, in th...* London: John Murray. 1826. 260 p.

> Engravings from drawings by Rober... teen plates of Hawaii, one of *Blonde's* trad...

77. GREEN, JONATHAN S. *Journal of a Tour on t... Coast of America in the year 1829....* New... Fred. Heartman. 1915. 105 p.

> No illustrations.

78. GREEN, MRS. J. S. "Extracts from a Journal Let... ship 'Parthian'...." In *The Friend,* vol. LXIII, Ju... p. 13–15.

> No illustrations.

79. HAY, SIR JOHN C. DALRYMPLE. *Lines from my Log-Bo...* Edinburgh: David Douglas. 1898. viii, 412 p.

> No illustrations of Hawaii, portrait of the author.

80. HILL, S. S. *Travels in the Sandwich and Society Islands.* London: Chapman and Hall. 1856. xii, 428 p.

> One map of Sandwich Islands.

80a. HILL, SAMUEL. "Voyage of the *Ophelia* ... Excerpts from the Journal of Captain Samuel Hill." Edited by James W. Snyder, Jr. In *The New England Quarterly,* vol. X, no. 2, June 1937, p. 355–380.

> No illustrations.

80b. HINDS, RICHARD BRINSLEY. "Journal of the Voyage of the *Sulphur* (1836–1842)." Transcribed and edited by E. Alison Kay, in *Hawaiian Journal of History,* vol. II, 1968, p. 102–135.

> Two illustrations of Hawaii by the author.

81. HINES, REV. GUSTAVUS. *Oregon: its History, Condition and Prospects: . . . during a residence of the author on the plains . . . while connected with the Oregon Mission....* Buffalo: Geo. H. Derby and Co. 1851. 437 p.

> Portrait of Hines.

> Other editions are in the library.

in 1805 and 1806," in *Forty-sixth Annual Report of The Hawaiian Historical Society for the Year 1937*, p. 27–38. No illustrations.

85. HUNNEWELL, JAMES. "Voyage in the Brig *Bordeaux Packet*, Boston to Honolulu, 1817...," in *Papers of The Hawaiian Historical Society No. 8*, p. 3–18. Honolulu. 1895. No illustrations.

86. HUNNEWELL, JAMES. *Journal of the Voyage of the Missionary Packet, Boston to Honolulu, 1826*. Charlestown: Privately Printed. 1880. xxvii, 77 p.

Copies of rare original engravings, one of *Packet*, one of Hunnewell.

86a. HUSSEY, JOHN A., ed. *The Voyage of the Raccoon ... 1813–1814*. San Francisco: Book Club of California. 1958. xxvii, 36 p.

87. INGRAHAM, JOSEPH. "The Log of the Brig *Hope* called the *Hope's* Track among the Sandwich Islands...." *Hawaiian Historical Society Reprints, No. 3*. Honolulu. 1918. 36 p.

Illustrated by photographs of drawings in log.
A photostat of the portion of the log which deals with Hawaii is also in the library.

88. IRVING, WASHINGTON. *Astoria, or Anecdotes of an Enterprise beyond the Rocky Mountains*. Philadelphia: Carey, Lea and Blanchard. 1836. 2 v.

No illustrations.
The London edition of 1836 is also in the library.

89. ISELIN, ISAAC. *Journal of a Trading Voyage Around the World. 1805–1808*. New York: Press of McIlroy & Emmet. No date. 110 p.

No illustrations.

89a. JARMAN, ROBERT. *Journal of a Voyage to the South Seas in the Japan....* London: Longman and Co. and Charles Tilt. [1838]. 242 p.

No illustrations.

89b. JARVES, JAMES JACKSON. *Scenes and Scenery in the Sandwich Islands ... during the years 1837–1842*. Boston: James Munroe and Co. 1843. 341 p.

Four illustrations of Hawaii, one map.

90. JENKINS, JAMES. *Autobiography of James Jenkins, written for his grandchildren.* Oshkosh, Wisconsin: The Hicks Printing Co. 1889. 110 p.

No illustrations.

90a. JOHNSTON, LIEUT. JAMES D. *China and Japan: Being a Narrative of the Cruise of the U. S. Steam-frigate Powhatan in the years 1857, '58, '59, and '60. Including an Account of the Japanese Embassy to the United States.* Philadelphia: Charles Desilver. 1861. 448 p.

Portraits of the principal officials of the Japanese embassy.

91. JUDD, GERRIT P. *Pages from the Diary of G. P. Judd ... in the ship "Parthian" 1827–1828. . . .* Honolulu: Star-Bulletin. 1928. 96 p.

No illustrations.

92. JUDD, LAURA FISH. *Honolulu Sketches of the Life ... in the Hawaiian Islands from 1828 to 1861.* New York: Anson D. F. Randolph & Co. 1880. xiv, 258 p.

Portrait of Mrs. Judd.

The edition of 1928 (Honolulu: Star-Bulletin) with a portrait of Dr. and Mrs. Judd is also in the library.

93. KELL, JOHN McINTOSH. *Recollections of a Naval Life. . . .* Washington: The Neale Co. 1900. 307 p.

No illustrations of Hawaii, portrait of Kell.

94. KOTZEBUE, OTTO VON. *Entdeckungs-Reise ... in den Jahren 1815, 1816, 1817 und 1818 ... auf dem schisse Rurick. . . .* Weimar: Hoffman. 1821. 3 v. in 1.

Two colored engravings of Hawaii, from original watercolors from Louis Choris.

95. KOTZEBUE, OTTO VON. *A Voyage of Discovery, ... in the years 1815–1818, ... in the ship Rurick. . . .* London: Longman, Hurst, Rees, Orme, and Brown. 1821. 3 v.

Two colored plates of Hawaii from original watercolors by Louis Choris in vol. I.

96. KOTZEBUE, OTTO VON. *A New Voyage Round the World, in the years 1823, 24, 25, and 26.* London: Henry Colburn and Richard Bentley. 1830. 2 v.

One engraving of Hawaii in vol. II from an original watercolor by Louis Choris.

81a. HOLMAN, LUCIA RUGGLES. *Journal.* . . . Bernice
Museum Special Publication 17. Honolulu: 19.
Portrait of author and her husband.

82. HOLMES, REV. LEWIS. *The Arctic Whaleman; or
the Arctic Ocean.* . . . Boston: Wentworth & C
296 p.
No illustrations of Hawaii.

83. HOOPER, W[ILLIAM] H[ULME]. *Ten Months Among
Tents of the Tuski.* . . . London: John Murray. 1853.
417 p.
No illustrations of Hawaii.

84. HOWAY, FREDERIC WILLIAM. "Early relations between the
Hawaiian Islands and the Northwest Coast," in *The
Hawaiian Islands . . . Papers read during the Captain
Cook Sesquicentennial Celebration, Honolulu, August
17, 1928.* Albert P. Taylor and Ralph S. Kuykendall,
editors. Honolulu: Archives of Hawaii, Publication No.
5. 1930. 93 p.
No illustrations.

84a. HOWAY, FREDERIC WILLIAM. "A List of Trading Vessels
in the Maritime Fur Trade, 1795 . . . to . . . 1825," in *The
Transactions of the Royal Society of Canada*, third series
section II, vol. XXIV–XXVIII. 1930–1934.
No illustrations.

84b. HOWAY, FREDERIC WILLIAM. "Last Days of the *Atahualpa*
alias *Bering*," in *Forty-first Annual Report of The H.
waiian Historical Society for the Year 1932.*
No illustrations.

84c. HOWAY, FREDERIC WILLIAM. "The ship *Eliza* at Haw
1799," in *Forty-second Annual Report of The Hau
Historical Society for the Year 1933*, p. 103–113.
No illustrations.

84d. HOWAY, FREDERIC WILLIAM. "The *Caroline* and the
cock at Hawaii in 1799," in *Forty-fifth Annual Rep
The Hawaiian Historical Society for the Year 19.
25–29.
No illustrations.

84e. HOWAY, FREDERIC WILLIAM. "The Ship *Pearl* in H

waii in 1818," translation by Joseph Barth, of extracts from tenth and eleventh chapters of Golovnin's *Tour Around the World.* . . . St. Petersburg, 1822. In *The Friend,* vol. LII, July and August 1894, p. 50–53, 60–62. No illustrations.

76. GRAHAM, MRS. MARIA, compiler. *Voyage of the H. M. S. Blonde to the Sandwich Islands, in the years 1824–25.* . . . London: John Murray. 1826. 260 p.
   Engravings from drawings by Robert Dampier. Thirteen plates of Hawaii, one of *Blonde's* track.

77. GREEN, JONATHAN S. *Journal of a Tour on the North West Coast of America in the year 1829.* . . . New York: Chas. Fred. Heartman. 1915. 105 p.
   No illustrations.

78. GREEN, MRS. J. S. "Extracts from a Journal Letter . . . on ship 'Parthian'. . . ." In *The Friend,* vol. LXIII, July 1906, p. 13–15.
   No illustrations.

79. HAY, SIR JOHN C. DALRYMPLE. *Lines from my Log-Books.* Edinburgh: David Douglas. 1898. viii, 412 p.
   No illustrations of Hawaii, portrait of the author.

80. HILL, S. S. *Travels in the Sandwich and Society Islands.* London: Chapman and Hall. 1856. xii, 428 p.
   One map of Sandwich Islands.

80a. HILL, SAMUEL. "Voyage of the *Ophelia* . . . Excerpts from the Journal of Captain Samuel Hill." Edited by James W. Snyder, Jr. In *The New England Quarterly,* vol. X, no. 2, June 1937, p. 355–380.
   No illustrations.

80b. HINDS, RICHARD BRINSLEY. "Journal of the Voyage of the *Sulphur* (1836–1842)." Transcribed and edited by E. Alison Kay, in *Hawaiian Journal of History,* vol. II, 1968, p. 102–135.
   Two illustrations of Hawaii by the author.

81. HINES, REV. GUSTAVUS. *Oregon: its History, Condition and Prospects: . . . during a residence of the author on the plains . . . while connected with the Oregon Mission.* . . . Buffalo: Geo. H. Derby and Co. 1851. 437 p.
   Portrait of Hines.
   Other editions are in the library.

70b. FREYCINET, ROSE DE SAULCES DE. *Journal of.* . . . Paris: Société d'Éditions Géographiques. 1927. 190 p.

One watercolor of Hawaii.

A portion of this journal, translated from the French by Victor S. K. Houston, was published in *Paradise of the Pacific,* November 1936 through April 1937.

71. *Friend, The.* A monthly paper edited by the Rev. S. C. Damon, D.D. Published since January 1843; bimonthly in 1845, 1846, 1847; suspended from May to September 1849 and from February 1851 to May 1852.

Arrivals and departures of vessels are included in each issue. Narratives of voyages reprinted in *The Friend* are indexed separately in this volume.

72. GELETT, CHARLES WETHERBY. . . . *A Life on the Ocean autobiography of Captain Charles Wetherby Gelett.* Reprinted by permission from *The Ojai,* a California newspaper of the early 1890s. Honolulu: Hawaiian Gazette Co. 1917. 119 p.

Portrait of Gelett.

73. GERSTAECKER, FREDRICH W. C. *Narrative of a Journey Round the World.* . . . New York: Harper & Brothers. 1855. 624 p.

No illustrations.

74. GILBERT, GEORGE. *The Death of Captain James Cook.* Hawaiian Historical Society Reprints, No. 5. Honolulu. 1926. 30 p.

No illustrations.

74a. GILMAN, WILLIAM HENRY. *Letters . . . while acting as secretary to Commodore John C. Long, commander of the U.S. Steam frigate Merrimac . . . 1857–1858.* Exeter, N.H. 1911. 96 p.

Portraits of Long and Gilman.

74b. GOLOVNIN, VASILII MIKHAILOVICH. *Puteshestvie Vokrug' Svieta, po Povelieniiu Gosudaria Imperatora Sovershennoe, na Voennom' Shliupie Kamchatkie v' 1817, 1818 i 1819 Godakh', Flota Kapitanom' Golovniniem'.* Saint Petersburg: V Morskoi Tipografii. 1822. 2 v.

Chart of Honolulu harbor by Tabulevitch, 1818.

75. GOLOVNIN, VASILII MIKHAILOVICH. "Golovnin's Visit to Ha-

bound on a Voyage from Boston to the N. W. Coast and Sandwich Islands. Photostat of p. 242–245 of original in *Massachusetts Historical Collection,* 1st series, vol. 9, 1804.

No illustrations.

66. FARNHAM, T. J. *Life, Adventures, and Travels in California.* . . . Pictorial edition. New York: Nafis & Cornish, 1849. 468 p.

Five engravings of Hawaii.

67. FARNHAM, THOMAS J. *Travels in the Californias, and scenes in the Pacific Ocean.* New York: Saxton & Miles. 1844. 96 p.

No illustrations.

68. FLEURIEU, C. P. CLARET. *A Voyage Round the World, performed during the years 1790, 1791 and 1792 by Étienne Marchand.* . . . Translated from the French of Fleurieu. London: Printed for T. N. Longman, etc. 1801. 2 v.

No illustrations.

69. FRANCHERE, GABRIEL. *Narrative of a Voyage to the Northwest Coast of America in the years 1811, 1812, 1813, and 1814.* . . . Edited and translated from the original French edition of 1820 by J. V. Huntington. New York: J. S. Redfield. 1854. 376 p.

No engravings of Hawaii.

A reprint of this 1854 edition may be found in Reuben Gold Thwaites: *Early Western Travels: 1748–1846,* vol. VI, 1904.

69a. FRANCHERE, GABRIEL. *Adventure at Astoria, 1810–1814.* Translated and edited by Hoyt C. Franchere. Norman, Okla.: University of Oklahoma Press. 1967. xxxix, 190 p.

No illustrations of Hawaii; portrait of Franchere.

70. FRANKLIN, SAMUEL R. *Memories of a Rear-Admiral.* . . . New York: Harper & Brothers. 1898. 398 p.

No illustrations of Hawaii, portrait of Franklin.

70a. FREYCINET, LOUIS DE. *Voyage Autour du Monde, . . . Exécuté sur les Corvettes de L. M. l'Uranie et la Physicienne, pendant les années 1817, 1819 et 1820.* . . . Vol. II. Paris: Chez Pillett Aine. 1829.

No illustrations.

in 1805 and 1806," in *Forty-sixth Annual Report of The Hawaiian Historical Society for the Year 1937*, p. 27–38. No illustrations.

85. HUNNEWELL, JAMES. "Voyage in the Brig *Bordeaux Packet*, Boston to Honolulu, 1817. . . ," in *Papers of The Hawaiian Historical Society No. 8*, p. 3–18. Honolulu. 1895. No illustrations.

86. HUNNEWELL, JAMES. *Journal of the Voyage of the Missionary Packet, Boston to Honolulu, 1826.* Charlestown: Privately Printed. 1880. xxvii, 77 p.

Copies of rare original engravings, one of *Packet*, one of Hunnewell.

86a. HUSSEY, JOHN A., ed. *The Voyage of the Raccoon . . . 1813–1814.* San Francisco: Book Club of California. 1958. xxvii, 36 p.

87. INGRAHAM, JOSEPH. "The Log of the Brig *Hope* called the *Hope's* Track among the Sandwich Islands. . . ." *Hawaiian Historical Society Reprints, No. 3.* Honolulu. 1918. 36 p.

Illustrated by photographs of drawings in log.

A photostat of the portion of the log which deals with Hawaii is also in the library.

88. IRVING, WASHINGTON. *Astoria, or Anecdotes of an Enterprise beyond the Rocky Mountains.* Philadelphia: Carey, Lea and Blanchard. 1836. 2 v.

No illustrations.

The London edition of 1836 is also in the library.

89. ISELIN, ISAAC. *Journal of a Trading Voyage Around the World. 1805–1808.* New York: Press of McIlroy & Emmet. No date. 110 p.

No illustrations.

89a. JARMAN, ROBERT. *Journal of a Voyage to the South Seas in the Japan. . . .* London: Longman and Co. and Charles Tilt. [1838]. 242 p.

No illustrations.

89b. JARVES, JAMES JACKSON. *Scenes and Scenery in the Sandwich Islands . . . during the years 1837–1842.* Boston: James Munroe and Co. 1843. 341 p.

Four illustrations of Hawaii, one map.

111

90. JENKINS, JAMES. *Autobiography of James Jenkins, written for his grandchildren.* Oshkosh, Wisconsin: The Hicks Printing Co. 1889. 110 p.

   No illustrations.

90a. JOHNSTON, LIEUT. JAMES D. *China and Japan: Being a Narrative of the Cruise of the U. S. Steam-frigate Powhatan in the years 1857, '58, '59, and '60. Including an Account of the Japanese Embassy to the United States.* Philadelphia: Charles Desilver. 1861. 448 p.

   Portraits of the principal officials of the Japanese embassy.

91. JUDD, GERRIT P. *Pages from the Diary of G. P. Judd ... in the ship "Parthian" 1827–1828....* Honolulu: Star-Bulletin. 1928. 96 p.

   No illustrations.

92. JUDD, LAURA FISH. *Honolulu Sketches of the Life ... in the Hawaiian Islands from 1828 to 1861.* New York: Anson D. F. Randolph & Co. 1880. xiv, 258 p.

   Portrait of Mrs. Judd.

   The edition of 1928 (Honolulu: Star-Bulletin) with a portrait of Dr. and Mrs. Judd is also in the library.

93. KELL, JOHN MCINTOSH. *Recollections of a Naval Life....* Washington: The Neale Co. 1900. 307 p.

   No illustrations of Hawaii, portrait of Kell.

94. KOTZEBUE, OTTO VON. *Entdeckungs-Reise ... in den Jahren 1815, 1816, 1817 und 1818 ... auf dem schisse Rurick....* Weimar: Hoffman. 1821. 3 v. in 1.

   Two colored engravings of Hawaii, from original watercolors from Louis Choris.

95. KOTZEBUE, OTTO VON. *A Voyage of Discovery, ... in the years 1815–1818, ... in the ship Rurick....* London: Longman, Hurst, Rees, Orme, and Brown. 1821. 3 v.

   Two colored plates of Hawaii from original watercolors by Louis Choris in vol. I.

96. KOTZEBUE, OTTO VON. *A New Voyage Round the World, in the years 1823, 24, 25, and 26.* London: Henry Colburn and Richard Bentley. 1830. 2 v.

   One engraving of Hawaii in vol. II from an original watercolor by Louis Choris.

97. KRUSENSTERN, ADAM JOHN VON. *Voyage Round the World, in the Years 1803, 1804, 1805, & 1806 ... on board the ships Nadeshda and Neva....* Translated from the original German by Richard B. Hoppner. London: John Murray. 1813. 2 v. in 1.
No illustrations of Hawaii.
Other volumes about von Krusenstern are in the library.

98. KUYKENDALL, RALPH S., and GREGORY, HERBERT E. *A History of Hawaii.* New York: Macmillan Co. 1926. 375 p.
Illustrations of Hawaii.

98a. KUYKENDALL, RALPH S. *The Hawaiian Kingdom.* Honolulu: University of Hawaii Press. 1938–1967. 3 v.
Illustrated.

99. LAFOND, GABRIEL. *Voyages Autour Du Monde et Naufrages Célèbres....* Paris: Administration de Librarie. 1843–1844. 8 v. in 4.
Two engravings of Hawaii in vol. IV.

100. LA GRAVIÊRE, JURIEN DE. *Voyage en Chine ... pendant les années 1847–1848–1849–1850.* Paris: Charpentier. 1854. 2 v.
No illustrations of Hawaii.

101. LANGSDORFF, GEORGE HENRY VON. *Voyages and Travels in Various Parts of the World, during the years 1803, 1804, 1805, 1806, and 1807.* Carlisle: George Philips, etc. 1817. 617, [17] p.
No illustrations of Hawaii.
Other editions are in the library.

102. LA PÉROUSE, J. F. G. DE. *Voyage de la Pérouse autour du monde ...* Rédigé par M. S. A. Milet-Mureau. Paris: Plassan. 1798. 4 v.
No illustrations.

103. LA PÉROUSE. J. F. G. DE. *The Voyage of La Pérouse Round the World, in the years 1785, 1786, 1787, and 1788....* Translated from the French. London: John Stockdale. 1798. 2 v.
No engravings of Hawaii.

104. LA PÉROUSE, J. F. G. DE. *A Voyage Round the World, performed in the years 1785, 1786, 1787, and 1788 by the*

 Boussole and Astrolabe. . . . London: Printed by A. Hamilton for G. G. and J. Robinson, etc. 1799. 2 v. and atlas.

 One view of Hawaii by Blondella, and map of the Sandwich Islands, in the atlas. Portrait of La Pérouse in vol. I.

105. LAPLACE, M. *Campagne de Circumnavigation de la frégate l'Artémise, pendant les années 1837, 1838, 1839 et 1840* . . . Publié par ordre du Roi. . . . Paris: Arthus Bertrand 1841–1854. 6 v.

 One engraving of Hawaii in vol. V; one of *Artémise* in vol. I.

106. LA SALLE, A————— DE. *Voyage Autour Du Monde exécuté pendant les années 1836 et 1837 sur la corvette La Bonite commandée par M. Vaillant . . . Relation Du Voyage.* Paris: Arthus Bertrand. 1845–1852. 3 v.

 No illustrations.

 Copies of the books written by the scientific members of this expedition are in the library, and are omitted from this list because they are not "historical narratives."

107. LAY, WILLIAM, and HUSSEY, CYRUS. *A Narrative of the Mutiny, on board the Ship Globe, of Nantucket, in the Pacific Ocean, Jan. 1824.* . . . New London: Published by Wm. Lay and C. M. Hussey. 1828. 168 p.

 No illustrations.

 The reprint issued by the Abbey Press "of New York, London, Montreal, and elsewhere" also is in the library.

108. LEDYARD, JOHN. *A Journal of Capt. Cook's Last Voyage to the Pacific Ocean . . . Performed in the years 1776, 1777, 1778, and 1779.* Hartford: Nathaniel Patten. 1783. 208 p.

 Chart showing ships' tracks.

109. LEE, D., and FROST, J. H. *Ten Years in Oregon.* New York: Published for the authors. J. Collord, Printer. 1844. 344 p.

 No engravings of Hawaii.

109a. LE NETREL, EDMOND. *Voyage of the Héros around the World with Duhaut-Cilly in the Years 1826 . . . 1829.* . . . Translated by Blanche Collett Wagner. Los Angeles: Glen Dawson. 1951. 64 p.

 One illustration of Hawaii.

110. LISIANSKY, UREY. *A Voyage Round the World, in the years*

1803, 4, 5, & 6; . . . in the ship Neva. London: John Booth, etc. 1814. xxi, 388 p.

No illustrations of Hawaii, portrait of Lisiansky, chart of voyage.

111. LITTLE, GEORGE. *Life on the Ocean, or Twenty Years at Sea.* . . . Baltimore: Armstrong & Berry. 1843. 395 p.

No illustrations of Hawaii.

Later editions are also in the library.

111a. LIVINGSTON-LITTLE, D. E., ed. "A Scotsman Views Hawaii: An 1852 Log of a Cruise of the *Emily Bourne*," [probable author, JOHN SHEDDON DAVIS]. Annotation by Edward Joesting, in *Journal of the West*, vol. IX, no. 2, April 1970, p. 196–221.

No illustrations.

112. LOOMIS, MRS. MARIA. "Journal of Mrs. Maria Southworth Loomis." Typewritten copy. 200 p.

No illustrations.

113. LOW, CAPT. CHARLES P. *Some Recollections . . . 1847–1873.* Boston: Geo. H. Ellis Co. 1906. 179 p.

Portrait of Low.

114. [LUCATT, EDWARD]. *Rovings in the Pacific from 1837 to 1849.* . . . London: Longman, Brown, Green, and Longmans. 1851. 2 v.

No illustrations of Hawaii.

114a. LYMAN, ALBERT. *Journal of a Voyage to California and . . . to the Sandwich Islands.* Hartford, Conn.: E. T. Pease. 1852. 183 p.

No illustrations.

115. LYMAN, CHESTER S. *Around the Horn to the Sandwich Islands and California 1845–1850.* . . . Edited by Frederick J. Teggart. New Haven: Yale University Press. 1924. xviii, 328 p.

Five photographs of Hawaii, two portraits of Lyman.

A typewritten copy of Mss. of Lyman's Hawaiian Journals is in the library.

115a. LYMAN, SARAH JOINER. . . . *Her Own Story.* Compiled by Margaret Greer Martin. Hilo, Hawaii: Lyman House Museum. 1970. 201 p.

Portraits of the Lyman family; scenes on Island of Hawaii.

116. MACRAE, JAMES. *With Lord Byron at the Sandwich Islands in 1825. Being extracts from the MS. diary of James Macrae, Scottish botanist.* Edited by W. F. Wilson. Honolulu: 1922. 75 p.

Illustrated by photographs.

116a. MANBY, THOMAS. "Journal of Vancouver's Voyage to the Pacific Ocean (1791–1793)," in *The Honolulu Mercury,* June through August 1929.

No illustrations.

117. MARTIN, JOHN, M. D. *An Account of the Natives of the Tongan Islands... Arranged from the extensive communications of Mr. William Mariner....* Second edition, with additions. London: John Murray. 1818. 2 v.

No illustrations of Hawaii.

Two other editions are in the library.

118. MASSETT, STEPHEN C. *"Drifting About,"* or what *"Jeems Pipes of Pipesville"* saw and did. New York: Carleton. 1863. 371 p.

One comic illustration of Hawaii.

119. MATHISON, GILBERT FARQUHAR. *Narrative of a Visit to Brazil, Chile, Peru and the Sandwich Islands, during the years 1821 and 1822....* London: Printed for Charles Knight. 1825. xii, 478 p.

One chart of Sandwich Islands, two colored prints of Hawaii.

120. MAYNE, RICHARD CHARLES. *Four Years in British Columbia and Vancouver Island....* London: John Murray. 1862. xi, 468 p.

One vignette of Hawaii.

121. MEARES, JOHN. *Mr. Mears's Memorial, dated 30th April 1790. With 14 enclosures.* Ordered to be printed 13th May 1790. 31 p.

No illustrations.

122. MEARES, JOHN. *Voyages... faits dans les années 1788 et 1789; précédés de la relation d'un autre voyage exécuté en 1786 sur le vaisseau le Nootka....* Paris: Chez F. Buisson. 1795. 3 v. and atlas.

Two engravings of Hawaii, portrait of Meares, one chart of voyages, all in atlas.

123. MEARES, JOHN. *Voyages Made in the Years 1788 and 1789 ... to which are prefixed ... a voyage performed in 1786 ... in the ship Nootka....* London: Logographic Press. 1790. viii, [12], 372, [108] p.

Two engravings of Hawaii, portrait of Meares, one chart of voyage.

124. MELVIN, JOHN L. *A Narrative of a Voyage Round the World commenced in 1816, and ended in 1824....* Georgetown, D. C. 1825. 28 p.

No illustrations.

Only a typewritten copy of Hawaiian portion in this library.

125. MENZIES, ARCHIBALD. *Hawaii Nei 128 Years Ago.* Edited by W. F. Wilson. Honolulu: The New Freedom Press. 1920. viii, 199 p.

Many illustrations, portrait of Menzies.

126. MEYEN, DR. F. J. F. *Reise um die Erde ... auf Prinzess Louise commandirt von Capitain W. Wendt in den Jahren 1830, 1831, und 1832.* Berlin: In der Sander'schen Buchhandlung. 1834. 2 v.

No illustrations of Hawaii.

127. MEYEN, DR. F. J. F. "Voyage round the World in the Prussian Ship the *Princess Louise,*" in *The Foreign Quarterly Review,* vol. XV, p. 1–24. American edition. New York: Theodore Foster. 1835.

No illustrations.

127a. MEYERS, WILLIAM H. *Journal of a Cruise to California and the Sandwich Islands in the United States Sloop-of-War Cyane....* Edited by John Haskell Kemble. San Francisco: Book Club of California. 1955. 68 p.

Three watercolors of Hawaii by the author.

128. *Minutes of General Meetings, 1830–1853.* Two vols. of bound pamphlets, being records of the annual meetings of the Sandwich Island Mission.

129. *Missionary Herald, The.* A magazine published in Massachusetts to stimulate interest in missions. Portions for the

years 1820–1891 which deal with the Hawaiian Islands are in the library.

130. MORRELL, CAPT. BENJAMIN, JUN. *A Narrative of Four Voyages . . . from the year 1822 to 1831. . . .* New York: J. and J. Harper. 1832. 492 p.

Portrait of Morrell.

131. MORTIMER, LIEUT. GEORGE. *Observations and Remarks made during a voyage . . . in the brig Mercury. . . .* London: Printed for the author and sold by T. Cadell, etc. 1791. viii, [8], 71 p.

No engravings of Hawaii.

Other editions are in the library.

132. MULLET, J. C. *A Five Years' Whaling Voyage.* Weymouth: D. Archer's Royal Library. 1863. 80 p.

No illustrations.

132a. MURAGAKI AWAJI-NO-KAMI. *Kokai Nikki. The Diary of the First Japanese Embassy to the United States of America.* Translated from the Japanese and compiled by Helen M. Uno. Tokyo: Foreign Affairs Association of Japan. 1958. 209 p.

One watercolor of Hawaii, sketches of the *Powhatan* and *Kanrin Maru.*

133. MURRELL, WILLIAM MEACHAM. *Cruise of the Frigate Columbia around the world . . . in 1838, 1839, and 1840.* Boston: Benjamin B. Mussey. 1840. 230 p.

No illustrations.

134. MYERS, JOHN. *The Life, Voyages and Travels of Capt. John Myers, detailing his adventures during four voyages round the world. . . .* London: Longman, Hurst, Rees and Co. 1817. 410 p.

No illustrations.

135. NEVENS, WILLIAM. *Forty Years at Sea: or a narrative of the adventures of William Nevens. . . .* Portland: Thurston, Fenley & Co., Printers. 1846. 314 p.

No engravings of Hawaii.

135a. NEWELL, ROBERT ROSE. *Two Brothers. Narrative of a Voyage around the World in the Bark "Sea Breeze," Captain George Newell, 1850 . . . with descriptive passages on . . .*

Captain Fisher A. Newell. Norwalk, Conn.: privately printed. 1961. xiii, 97 p.

Two pen-and-ink sketches of Hawaii "from old prints."

136. NICOL, JOHN. *The Life and Adventures of John Nicol, Mariner.* Edinburgh: William Blackwood. 1822. viii, 215 p.

Portrait of John Nicol.

137. [OLIVER, JAMES]. *Wreck of the Glide, with Recollections of the Fijiis, and of Wallis Island.* New York: Wiley and Putnam. 1848. 203 p.

No illustrations of Hawaii.

The 1846 edition in the library was not used because it is not complete.

138. OLMSTED, FRANCIS ALLYN. *Incidents of a Whaling Voyage.* ... New York: D. Appleton and Co. 1841. 360 p.

Four lithographs of Hawaii, one of the *North America.*

139. OSBORN, SHERARD. *The Discovery of the North-west Passage by H.M.S. Investigator, Capt. R. M'Clure, 1850, 1851, 1852, 1853, 1854.* Second edition. London: Longman, Brown, Green, Longmans, & Roberts. 1857. xxxii, 463 p.

No illustrations of Hawaii.

140. PARKER, REV. SAMUEL. *Journal of an Exploring Tour beyond the Rocky Mountains, under . . . the A.B.C.F.M. in the years 1835, '36, and '37.* . . . Third edition. Ithaca, N.Y.: Mack, Andrus, & Woodruff. 1842. 408 p.

No engravings of Hawaii.

The library has two other editions.

141. PATTERSON, SAMUEL. *Narrative of the Adventures and Sufferings of Samuel Patterson.* . . . From the press in Palmer. 1817. 144 p.

No illustrations.

Another edition of the above with the title page missing is in the library.

142. PAULDING, LIEUT. HIRAM. *Journal of a Cruise of the United States Schooner Dolphin . . . in pursuit of the mutineers of the whale ship Globe.* New York: G. & C. & H. Carvil. 1831. 258 p.

No illustrations.

143. PERKINS, EDWARD T. *Na Motu; or, Reef-Rovings in the South Seas.* . . . New York: Pudney & Russell. 1854. 456 p.
    Five lithographs of Hawaii, one map.

144. PÉRON. *Mémoires du Capitaine Péron, sur ses voyages.* . . . Paris: Brissot-Thivars. 1824. 2 v.
    No engravings of Hawaii.

144a. PIERCE, RICHARD A. *Russia's Hawaiian Adventure, 1815–1817.* Berkeley: University of California Press. 1965. 245 p.
    No illustrations.

145. *Polynesian, The.* A weekly journal, edited by J. J. Jarves. First series, from June 6, 1840 to December 4, 1841. Second series, from May 1844. Discontinued 1862.

146. PORTER, DAVID. *Journal of a Cruise Made to the Pacific Ocean, by Capt. David Porter, in the United States Frigate Essex in the Years 1812, 1813, and 1814.* . . . Second edition. New York: Wiley & Halsted. 1822. 2 v.
    No engravings of Hawaii.

147. PORTLOCK, CAPT. NATHANIEL. *A Voyage Round the World* . . . *performed in 1785, 1786, 1787, and 1788.* . . . London: John Stockdale and George Goulding. 1789. xii, 384, xl p.
    Four engravings of Hawaii, portrait of Portlock.
    Other books concerning this voyage are in the library.

148. QUARTER MASTER, OLD [JOHN BECHERVAISE]. *Thirty-six Years of a Seafaring Life.* Portsea: W. Woodward. 1839. 336 p.
    No illustrations.

148a. QUIMPER, BENITEZ DEL PINO, MANUEL. *The Sandwich Islands.* . . . Madrid: E. Aguado. 1822. Translated from the Spanish by Clark Lee, Honolulu, 1937. Typed copy, 27 p.
    No illustrations.

149. REYNOLDS, J. N. *Voyage of the United States Frigate Potomac* . . . *in the years 1831, 1832, 1833, and 1834.* . . . New York: Harper & Brothers. 1835. 560 p.
    No illustrations of Hawaii.

149a. REYNOLDS, STEPHEN. *The Voyage of the New Hazard* . . .

1810–1813.... Edited by Judge F. W. Howay. Salem: Peabody Museum. 1938. xxii, 158 p.

One painting of *New Hazard* by George Ropes of Salem, and one of Honolulu harbor in 1821 by C. E. Bensell. Portrait of Reynolds by J. M. Stanley, Honolulu, 1848.

150. [RICKMAN, JOHN]. *Journal of Captain Cook's Last Voyage ...performed in the years 1776, 1777, 1778, 1779.* Faithfully narrated from the original Ms. Dublin: printed for Messrs. Price, Whitestone, etc. 1781. xlvii, 396 p.

One engraving of Hawaii.

The second edition (London, 1781) is also in the library.

151. ROQUEFEUIL, M. CAMILLE DE. *A Voyage Round the World between the years 1816–1819.* London: Sir Richard Phillips and Co. 1823. 112 p.

No illustrations.

152. ROSEN, W. VON. *Steen Bille's Bericht über die Reise der Corvette Galathea ... in den Jahren 1845, 46 und 47.* Copenhagen: C. A. Reitzel. 1852. 2 v.

Three scenes of Hawaii by August Plum in vol. II.

153. ROSEN, W. VON. *Steen Bille's Report of the voyage of the corvette Galathea ... in the years 1845, 46 and 47.* Translated into English from W. von Rosen's German edition. Typewritten Mss. 226 p.

No illustrations.

154. ROSS, ALEXANDER. *Adventures of the First Settlers on the Oregon or Columbia River....* London: Smith, Elder and Co. 1849. xv, 352 p.

No illustrations.

Other editions are in the library.

155. ROVING PRINTER, A. *Life and Adventure in the South Pacific.* New York: Harper & Brothers. 1861. 361 p.

One engraving, one chart of Hawaii.

155a. RUGGLES, SAMUEL and NANCY. "From a Missionary Journal," in *The Atlantic Monthly*, vol. 134, November 1924, p. 648–657.

No illustrations.

156. RUSCHENBERGER, W. S. W. *Narrative of a Voyage Round the World, during the years 1835, 36, and 37....* London: Richard Bentley. 1838. 2 v.
No illustrations of Hawaii.

157. SAMWELL, DAVID. *A Narrative of the Death of Captain James Cook.* Hawaiian Historical Society Reprints No. 2. Honolulu: [1917]. 26 p.
Portrait of Cook.

158. *Sandwich Island Gazette and Journal of Commerce.* Edited by S. D. Mackintosh. Weekly from August 1836 to July 1839. Honolulu.

159. SEEMANN, BERTHOLD. *Narrative of the Voyage of H.M.S. Herald during the years 1845–51....* London: Reeve and Co. 1853. 2 v.
Chart of voyage, lithograph of *Herald* and *Plover*, no illustrations of Hawaii.

160. SHALER, WILLIAM. "Journal of a Voyage Between China and the North-Western Coast of America, made in 1804," in *American Register...*, vol. III, p. 137–175. Philadelphia: C. and A. Conrad and Co. 1808.
No illustrations.

161. SHAW, WILLIAM. *Golden Dreams and Waking Realities....* London: Smith, Elder and Co. 1851. xii, 316 p.
No illustrations.

162. SIMPSON, SIR GEORGE. *Narrative of a Journey Round the World, during the years 1841 and 1842.* London: Henry Colburn. 1847. 2 v.
Map of route, portrait of Simpson.
The Philadelphia edition of 1847 is also in the library.

163. SKOGMAN, C. *Erdumsegelung der Königl Schwedischen Fregatte Eugenie. In den Jahren 1851 bis 1853 ... unter ... Commandeur-Capitains C. A. Virgin....* Translated by Anton von Etzel from the Swedish of Skogman. Berlin: Otto Janke. 1856. 2 v. in 1.
Four colored lithographs of Hawaii.
The Berlin edition of 1857 is also in the library.

163a. SKOGMAN, C. "His Swedish Majesty's Frigate *Eugenie* at Honolulu, 22 June–2 July, 1852," being a reprint of seventeen pages from *Fregatten Eugenies Resa Omkring Jor-*

den, åren 1851–1853, under Befäl af C. A. Virgin. Translated from the original Swedish by Meiric K. Dutton. Honolulu: Loomis House Press. 1954. [21 p.]
   Map of track of *Eugenie.*

164. SLADE, JOHN. ... *Old Slade; or, Fifteen years adventures of a sailor.* ... Boston: John Putnam. c. 1844. 108 p.
   Portrait of Slade, no illustrations of Hawaii.

165. SNOW, SAMUEL. *The Exile's Return: or a narrative of Samuel Snow, who was banished to Van Dieman's Land, for participating in the patriot war in Upper Canada in 1838.* Cleveland: Smead & Cowles. 1849. 32 p.
   No illustrations of Hawaii.

166. STEEN BILLE. See entry 19a BILLE, STEEN ANDERSON.

167. STEVENS, BENJAMIN F. *A Cruise on the Constitution Around the world on old Ironsides 1844–1847.* New York: Reprinted from "The United Service Magazine." 1904. 67 p.
   No illustrations.

168. STEWART, C. S. *Private Journal of a Voyage to the Pacific Ocean, and Residence at the Sandwich Islands in the years 1822, 1823, 1824, and 1825.* New York: John P. Haven. 1828. 406 p.
   Six lithographs of Hawaii, one of *Thames,* one map.
   Later editions are also in the library.

169. STEWART, C. S. *A Visit to the South Seas, in the U.S. Ship Vincennes, during the years 1829 and 1830.* ... New York: John P. Haven. 1831. 2 v.
   No illustrations.
   The London edition of 1832 in this library has a portrait of Stewart.

169a. TALBOT, THEODORE. *The Journals of ... with the First Military Company in Oregon Territory, 1849–1852.* Edited with Notes by Charles H. Carey. Portland, Ore.: Metropolitan Press. 1931. 153 p.
   No illustrations.

170. TAYLOR, FITCH W. *The Flag Ship: or a voyage around the world, in the United States Frigate Columbia.* ... New York: D. Appleton & Co. 1840. 2 v.
   No illustrations of Hawaii.

The third edition (New Haven, 1844) is also in the library.

171. THIERCELIN, LE DR. *Journal d'un Baleinier voyages en océanie.* Paris: L. Hachette & Co. 1866. 2 v.
No illustrations.

172. THURSTON, LUCY G. *Life and Times of Mrs. Lucy G. Thurston....* Selected and arranged by herself. Ann Arbor, Mich.: S. C. Andrews. 1882. x, 307 p.
Portrait of Mrs. Thurston.
The second edition of 1921 is also in the library.

173. TORREY, WILLIAM. *Torrey's Narrative: or, the Life and Adventures of William Torrey....* Written by himself. Boston: A. J. Wright. 1848. 300 p.
No illustrations of Hawaii, portrait of Torrey.

174. TOWNSEND, EBENEZER, JR. "The Diary of Mr. Ebenezer Townsend, Jr. the Supercargo of the Sealing Ship 'Neptune.' ...." *Papers of the New Haven Colony Historical Society,* vol. IV, p. 1–115. New Haven, Conn. 1888.
No illustrations.
The Hawaiian Historical Society's reprint of the portion of this diary dealing with Hawaii is in the library.

175. TOWNSEND, JOHN K. *Narrative of a Journey Across the Rocky Mountains ... and a visit to the Sandwich Islands. ...* Philadelphia: Henry Perkins. 1839. 352 p.
No illustrations.

176. TURNBULL, JOHN. *A Voyage Round the World, in the years 1800, 1801, 1802, 1803, and 1804....* Second edition. London: Published by A. Maxwell, etc. 1813. xv, 516 p.
No illustrations.
The library also has the first edition which omits the dates of Turnbull's visit to Hawaii.

177. TYERMAN, DANIEL, and BENNET, GEORGE. *Journal of Voyages and Travels by ... D. Tyerman and G. Bennet ... between the years 1821 and 1829.* Compiled from original documents by James Montgomery. London: Frederick Westley and A. H. Davis. 1831. 2 v.
One engraving of Hawaii, portraits of Tyerman and Bennet.
Two other editions are in the library.

178. VANCOUVER, GEORGE. *A Voyage of Discovery to the North Pacific Ocean ... performed in the years 1790, 1791, 1792, 1793, 1794, and 1795, in the Discovery ... and ... Chatham....* London: G. G. and J. Robinson and J. Edwards. 1798. 3 v. and atlas.

   One view of Hawaii in vol. III, three views and a chart of the Sandwich Islands in the atlas. Artists: Thomas Heddington and J. Sykes.

   One engraving of Hawaii in vol. III.

179. VANCOUVER, GEORGE. *A Voyage of Discovery to the North Pacific Ocean ... performed in the years 1790, 1791, 1792, 1793, 1794 and 1795, in the Discovery ... and ... Chatham....* A new edition, with corrections. London: John Stockdale. 1801. 6 v.

   One view of Hawaii by Thomas Heddington in vol. V.

   Also in the library is a French edition, 3 vols. and an atlas.

180. VAN DENBURGH, MRS. ELIZABETH DOUGLAS TURRILL. *My Voyage in the United States Frigate "Congress."* New York: Desmond FitzGerald, Inc. c. 1913. 338 p.

   Several photographs pertaining to this voyage.

180a. VARIGNY, CHARLES VICTOR CROSNIER DE. *Quatorze Ans Aux Iles Sandwich.* Paris: Librarie Hachette et cie. 1874. 350 p.

   No illustrations. Map of Hawaiian Islands.

181. VASSAR, JOHN GUY. *Twenty Years Around the World.* A third edition. New York: G. W. Carleton and Co. 1878. x, 598 p.

   No engravings of Hawaii, portrait of author.

181a. *Voyage Autour Du Monde ... 1836 et 1837 sur la Corvette La Bonite, Commandee par M. Vaillant....* Album Historique. Arthus Bertrand, éditeur. Paris: Librairie de la Société de Géographie. n.d. 100 plates.

   Six lithographs of Hawaii, three from drawings by Barthelme Lauvergne, and three from drawings by Théodore Auguste Fisquet.

   For an account of the voyage of the *Bonite,* see entry 106.

182. *Voyage Through the Islands of the Pacific Ocean, A.* Compiled from the most authentic and recent authorities. [Based on James Morris' account of *Arrow's* voyage.] Dublin: Bentham and Gardiner. 1824. 179 p.

One vignette of Hawaii.

The revised edition (New York, 1838) is also in the library.

183. WALPOLE, LIEUT. THE HON. FRED., R. N. *Four Years in the Pacific in Her Majesty's Ship "Collingwood" from 1844 to 1848.* London: Richard Bentley. 1849. 2 v.

One vignette of Hawaii in vol. 2.

The library also has the Paris edition of 1850.

184. WARREN, MRS. JANE S. *The Morning Star: History of the Children's Missionary Vessel and of the Marquesan and Micronesian Missions.* Boston: American Tract Society. 1860. 309 p.

Two vignettes of Hawaii, several of *Morning Star.*

185. WARREN, T. ROBINSON. *Dust and Foam; or, Three Oceans and Two Continents....* New York: Charles Scribner. 1859. xiii, 397 p.

No engravings of Hawaii.

186. WARRINER, FRANCIS. *Cruise of the United States Frigate Potomac round the world during the years 1831–34....* New York: Leavitt, Lord & Co. 1835. 366 p.

No illustrations of Hawaii.

187. WHEELER, DANIEL. *Extracts from the Letters and Journal of Daniel Wheeler....* London: Harvey and Darton. 1839. 300 p.

No illustrations.

Other books concerning Wheeler are in the library.

188. WHIDDEN, CAPT. JOHN D. *Ocean Life in the old sailing ship days.* Boston: Little, Brown & Co. 1908. xvi, 314 p.

No illustrations of Hawaii.

188a. WILCOX, ABNER and LUCY (HART). *Letters ... 1836–1869.* Edited by Ethel M. Damon. Honolulu: privately printed. 1950. 402 p.

Portraits of the authors; sketch of *Mary Frazier* and its accommodations.

189. WILKES, CHARLES. *Narrative of the United States Explor-*

ing *Expedition. During the years 1838, 1839, 1840, 1841, 1842.* Philadelphia: Lea & Blanchard. 1845. 5 v. and atlas.

Portrait of Wilkes in vol. I. Three illustrations of Hawaii in vol. III. One map and twenty-seven illustrations of Hawaii in vol. IV. From original sketches by Alfred T. Agate (draftsman and artist), T. R. Peale (naturalist), Joseph Drayton (naturalist), Wm. D. Brackenridge (horticulturist), and C. Wilkes, U.S.N. (commander of the expedition).

190. WILLIAMS, REV. EDWARD A. *The Cruise of the Pearl Round the World....* London: Richard Bentley. 1859. xii, 311 p.

No illustrations of Hawaii.

190a. WILSON, WILLIAM F. "Professor John Henry Anderson 'The Wizard of the North' at Honolulu in 1859," in *Forty-seventh Annual Report of The Hawaiian Historical Society for the Year 1938,* p. 50–70.

Portrait of Anderson.

191. WISE, HENRY AUGUSTUS. *Los Gringos: or an inside view of Mexico....* New York: Baker and Scribner. 1849. xvi, 453 p.

No illustrations.

The library has the New York edition of 1850.

192. WOOD, WM. MAXWELL, M. D. *Wandering Sketches... during a Cruise on Board the U.S. Ships Levant, Portsmouth, and Savannah.* Philadelphia: Carey and Hart. 1849. 386 p.

No illustrations.

192a. YANAGAWA MASAKIYO. *The First Japanese Mission to America (1960). Being a Diary kept by a member of the Embassy.* Translated from the Japanese by Junichi Fukuyama and Roderick H. Jackson. Edited with an introduction by M. C. Mori. New York: Fred A. Stokes. 1938. 85 p.

No illustrations of Hawaii.

193. ZIMMERMANN, HEINRICH. *...Zimmermann's Account of the Third Voyage of Captain Cook. 1776–1780.* Translated by Miss U. Tewsley. Alexander Turnbull Library.

Bulletin No. 2. Wellington: Government Printer. 1926. 49 p.

Chart of voyage, two photographs of old illustrations.

193a. ZIMMERMAN, HEINRICH. *Zimmerman's Captain Cook. An Account of the Third Voyage of Captain Cook around the World, 1776–1780. . . .* Translated from the Mannheim edition of 1781 by Elsa Michaelis and Cecil French. Edited with an introduction and notes by His Honour F. W. Howay. Toronto, Canada: Ryerson Press. [1930]. xiv, 120 p.

No illustrations; chart of Kealakekua Bay, Hawaii.

ABOUT THE AUTHORS

BERNICE JUDD was for thirty-three years librarian of the Hawaiian Mission Children's Society. As the great granddaughter of Dr. Gerrit P. Judd, medical missionary who voyaged to Hawaii in 1828 and later held important positions in the government of the Hawaiian Kingdom, she had a special interest in the early history of the Hawaiian Islands. After the printing of the first edition of this work in 1929, up until the time of her death in 1971, she kept copious notes on new materials for the second edition.

HELEN YONGE LIND has been associated with the Mission-Historical Library in a variety of capacities for sixteen years, including the position of secretary-librarian for The Hawaiian Historical Society. Her work on the original edition, which includes the addition of materials from the library of The Hawaiian Historical Society as well as from publications which became available after the printing of the first edition, has expanded the book by about one-third.